A STUDENT DIES,
A SCHOOL MOURNS

A STUDENT DIES, A SCHOOL MOURNS

Dealing with Death and Loss in the School Community

Ralph L. Klicker, Ph.D.

USA	Publishing Office	Accelerated Development A member of the Taylor & Francis Group 325 Chestnut Street, Suite 800 Philadelphia, PA 19106 Tel: (215) 625-8900 Fax: (215) 625-2940
	Distribution Center	Accelerated Development A member of the Taylor & Francis Group 7625 Empire Drive Florence, KY 41042 Tel: (800) 634-7064 Fax: (800) 248-4724
UK		Taylor & Francis 27 Church Road Hove E. Sussex BN3 2FA Tel: +44 (0) 1273 207411 Fax: +44 (0) 1273 205612

A STUDENT DIES, A SCHOOL MOURNS: Dealing with Death and Loss in the School Community

2   3   4   5   6   7   8   9   0

Printed by Braun-Brumfield, Ann Arbor, MI, 1999.
Cover design by Nancy Abbott. Images copyright Photo Disc, Inc., 1999.

A CIP catalog record for this book is available from the British Library.
∞ The paper in this publication meets the requirements of the ANSI Standard Z39.48-1984 (Permanence of Paper).

Library of Congress Cataloging-in-Publication Data

Klicker, Ralph L.
    A student dies, a school mourns : dealing with death and loss in
the school community / Ralph L. Klicker
        p.   cm.
    Includes bibliographical references and index.
    ISBN 1-56032-742-1 (pbk. : alk. paper)
    1. School crisis management—United States.   2. Students—United
States—Death—Psychological aspects.   3. Educational counseling—
United States.   4. Bereavement—United States—Psychological
aspects.   I. Title.
LB2866.5.K55   1999
371.4'6—dc21   99-30095
                                                      CIP

ISBN 1-56032-742-1 (paper)

*This book is dedicated to all individuals
who accept the responsibility of helping schools
through what is often the most tragic event
they will ever experience.*

CONTENTS

7

Helping Grieving Students   58

8

Teaching Students How to Behave in Grief-Related Situations   70

PREFACE

As I walked down the hall to the main office, I passed a male student sitting on the floor against his open locker, staring at the opposite wall. Two female students were hugging each other, crying. Students in a class were asking the teacher if it was true, that alcohol was involved. The teacher just shook her head and said, "I don't know."

In the main office, the telephones were ringing continuously, people with questions about the accident. The principal came out of his office with his arm around a man in shorts and sneakers who was wiping tears from his eyes. I assumed he was a coach. I introduced myself to the principal and heard another familiar response, "Thank God you're here. What should we do?" This question, "What should we do?" is the reason I wrote this book.

At the present time, there is an abundance of information available on death and dying. However, there is a limited amount of written or audio-visual material available that addresses the needs of a school community when one of its members dies. The available literature indicates that there is a need for school personnel to learn how the death of a student or staff member affects the school community. There is also a need for schools on all levels to develop an organized plan to respond to the death of a student or staff member. This plan should recognize the life of the person who died and facilitate the grieving process for those who are mourning.

This book is designed to be a systematic guide that incorporates a thorough analysis of grief in a school. It details normal and abnormal grief reactions, factors affecting these grief responses, and the differences in death beliefs and responses of students at different ages and developmental stages. It was also created to act as a map or step-by-step guide for establishing a death-related response plane.

The didactic possibilities of this book set it apart from others on the subject. A school can develop inservice training programs around it. The liberal use of flow charts, time tables and action plans turns the difficult task of creating a response plan into a relatively painless activity. Simply stated, the book explains what must be done, who should do it, and in what time period it should be done.

Extensive coverage is given to two topics of special interest to schools and mental health professions. Chapter 12 details an innovative and comprehensive method for dealing with suicide. Again, a step-by-step approach is taken in explaining responses to a suicide, warning signs, intervention strategies, and proven successful lesson plans for classroom instruction. Chapter 13 discusses the aftermath of violence and murder. One factor that makes this chapter unique is that it was written by a professor and grief specialist whose son was abducted at gun point, taken to a desolated area, shot in the head and left for dead. Miraculously, he survived and recovered. In this chapter, as throughout the entire book, the real-life experiences of the author shines through, making this an interesting, easy to read, and relevant text for educators, administrators, counselors, social workers, school psychologists, and students.

KNOWLEDGMENTS

I would like to thank Dr. Thomas Frantz for sharing, through his many years of experience, his knowledge of school interventions following a crisis.

I would also like to thank the following people and organizations for their contributions to this book:

Professor Patricia Evans, Niagara County Community College

Jane Emborsky, LPN, BS, Mental Health Association of Niagra County, Inc.

Jenifer Lawrence, MS, CRC, Mental Health Association of Niagra County, Inc.

Katherine Curro, Canton Central School System

The Virginia Department of Education

Special thanks are also extended to Carol Stadelmaier for typing the manuscript and Kristen Etu for intital editing and proofreading of the manuscript.

ACKNOWLEDGEMENTS

INTRODUCTION

"I've been shot by a crazy girl. Am I going to die?"

First grader Robert Trossman of Winnetka, Illinois, shot in the washroom, staggered through the hall into his classroom pleading in terror: "I've been shot by a crazy girl. Am I going to die?" (Spencer & Hilkewitch, 1998).

Death can take many forms when it strikes a school. It can be violent and unexpected, as it has been in Pearl, Mississippi; Jonesboro, Arkansas; Paducah, Kentucky; Edinboro, Pennsylvania; Taber, Alberta, Canada, and at the massacre in Littleton, Colorado's Columbine High School. Or it can be quiet and anticipated, as it was in Canton, New York, when middle school student Adam Crump died after a long illness.

Students and teachers are not immune to death or to the grief that follows it. The effect a death can have on the students and staff of a school can be as varied as the types of death that can strike it. Mass grief and mourning can sweep through a school following the death of a popular student or teacher, whereas the death of a not-so-well-known student, such as one who has recently transferred, may barely cause a ripple of response.

What students need most at this time is to be in a supportive, caring, and helpful environment. The school has a built-in support system of peers, teachers, counselors, and nurses. It is for this reason that whenever possible a school should remain open following a tragedy involving a death. It is not recommended that classes go on as usual, but they should be held. Instead of adhering to the normal lesson plans, they can be used for discussion, reflection, the expression of emotions, and mutual support.

Grieving in a school is not limited to students or to one level of school staff, such as the dead student's teachers. There can be grief responses exhibited throughout the entire staff, from bus drivers to principals. In one school, the bus driver had developed a good relationship with a student who died. She was very upset, whereas the principal, who did not personally know the student, was not as emotionally affected. At another school, the dead student was well known by the principal and her staff because he had worked in the office. At a third school, the school counselor was a neighbor of the dead student and was experiencing a grief response so intense that he was not able to take a leadership role in helping the school respond (Klicker, 1993).

Even staff members who would normally be expected to have the knowledge of how to respond to a school death are not always prepared. Counselors are given limited training, and sometimes none at all in the dynamics of grief and the school community. School psychologists, social workers, and counselors have contacted the author for suggestions on how to proceed when there was a school-related death.

The death of a member of the school community can have a devastating effect on the entire school. When the security of this "second home" is threatened by a death, the school must be prepared to provide an environment that encourages healthy grieving, an environment where students and staff feel free to express their emotions and share their feelings, and an environment that is sensitive to everyone's needs.

Crisis management, if it is to be effective, cannot be separated from the more traditional, academic components of the curriculum; nor can it be divorced from the community at large. General and special educators must be creative in developing crisis intervention techniques that combine their needs with those of students, parents, administrators, and other professionals (Obiakor, 1997).

Poland (1998) confirms the diverse groups of those in need when relating his intervention at the Westside Middle School in Jonesboro, Arkansas, in March 1998, where two students set up an ambush and killed one teacher and four students and wounded ten other students. In different meetings, his team met with 150 caregivers who came to help, including school staff, hospital personnel, students, and members of the press. Poland conducted an evening meeting of 500 people from the community. Parents were angry with the perpetrators, the state laws, and the system. Students had worries about returning to school, the bullet holes left in the walls, and re-entering their classrooms now that their teacher had been killed.

The key to being as helpful as possible to everyone involved is by being prepared for such a crisis before it occurs. Kline et al. (1995) state that if a school-related trauma is not adequately addressed at school, temporary disruption in the children's ability to concentrate can create a downward spiral in academic performance. Likewise, the way schools manage a crisis in the short term can negatively affect longer-term functioning. Staff morale and a school climate conducive to learning may be seriously impaired by an unaddressed or unresolved crisis situation.

Developing an emergency response plan is a way for school staff to think through the most appropriate steps to take in a crisis before one actually occurs. It allows for decisions to be made when there is time for rational, thoughtful planning, rather than in the heat of a tense moment (Preller, 1994). A poignant example of not being prepared is given by Lipton (1990) when he tells of a principal who denied that a murder had occurred in front of the school even though there was a covered body on the sidewalk and police were investigating. The next day, when the newspapers were full of the murder story, the students angrily confronted the principal for failing to deal appropriately with what had happened.

A crisis of major proportion calls for enlightened leadership: a take-charge manner combined with effective teamwork. Even with forethought, it may be difficult to think clearly under conditions of emotional arousal. Response behavior should be well learned and, ideally, practiced. Above all, the key is planning and preparation based on a modicum of specialized knowledge about school crisis (Lichtenstein et al., 1994).

Normal Grief

Grief is the normal, healthy, and appropriate response to loss for young children, adolescents, and adults. Although it is universal, everyone grieves in his own way. Most people associate grief with a loss through death, but grief can be experienced after any major loss. Events such as separation, divorce, relocation, or job loss can cause grief in a person's life.

Grief can be experienced from infancy to old age. Both the infant whose mother leaves him alone and the 90-year-old mother whose 70-year-old son dies experience grief. Even major changes and happy events can stimulate elements of grief. Graduating from one level of schooling to a higher level or starting a new career can mean leaving friends behind, which can cause grief responses.

Although everyone grieves differently, there are common responses that most children and adults experience. These can be classified under four categories: physical, mental, feeling, and spiritual. A bereaved individual (someone who has experienced a significant loss) will experience one or more of the following responses.

☐ Physical Responses

Although it is not exactly clear how the death of a significant person in our lives causes physical illness, it is generally believed that ill health may arise from an alteration in a person's immune system (Haig, 1990). Physical reactions that are common following a death or other major stressor in a person's life are:

- Stomach distress
- Difficulty breathing
- Muscle weakness
- Dry mouth
- Headache
- Chest pain or discomfort
- Change in bowel pattern
- Change in eating habits
- Lack of energy
- Nervousness
- Difficulty sleeping
- Overactivity
- Sighing
- Rash

Connelly (1992) has observed that there is an increase in reported visits to the school nurse following the death of a classmate or teacher. The reasons for the visits are for more non-specific symptoms such as not feeling well, headache, or stomach upset.

☐ Mental and Feeling Responses

When suffering through grief, people often feel helpless and out of control. The pain and confusion in their mental and feeling responses can be so intense that some truly believe they are "going crazy" (Kaczmarek, 1998). Mental responses include:

- Negative thoughts
- Confusion
- Difficulty concentrating
- Lower productivity
- Sleeplessness
- Forgetting details
- Mind going blank

Feeling responses include:

- Shock/disbelief/denial - Usually occurs with sudden deaths, but may also be seen with a prolonged illness. This is a defense mechanism to allow the person time to adjust to the situation. It is usually short-term.
- Sadness - Can be felt for the deceased for suffering they may have had or because they will no longer be able to experience life. Sadness is also felt for oneself and one's own loss.

- Loneliness - Even if the student has many other friends and is involved in different school, social, or family activities, he may still experience feelings of loneliness.
- Guilt - The guilt may be real or perceived. Often these feelings are exaggerated because the death does not allow the person to resolve the issue that caused the guilt with the deceased.
- Anger - Can be directed at the person for dying and leaving, at God for not preventing the death, toward other people, or even toward oneself.
- Anxiety - Can range from mild insecurity to intense panic. It may be caused by fear of one's own death or fear of how life will be without the deceased person.
- Crying - Whether considered a physical or emotional response, crying has a therapeutic value. It diminishes the negative effects of pent-up emotions and relieves stress.
- Preoccupation with thoughts of the deceased - This may cause absent-mindedness or the inability to concentrate. These thoughts may not only be of the past life with the deceased, but also fantasies about the deceased being alive in the future.
- Dreams/nightmares - Nightmares may be very distressful to a student and increase his feelings of guilt, fear, and anxiety. Pleasant dreams of the deceased may give the student a feeling of reassurance and calm.
- Confusing awake events - Although these are considered by many people to be paranormal or spiritual happenings, all have a firm foundation in reality and psychology. They include seeing or hearing the deceased or feeling as though the deceased is present or directing events.

☐ Spiritual Responses

The spiritual dimension for most children's grief responses involves a profound sense of loss at the death of a loved person and the ensuing struggle that follows to make sense of their feelings, including worry about the death of others whom they love (Irizarry, 1992). Spirituality can be affected by:

- Strengthening of a person's spiritual beliefs.
- Weakening of a person's spiritual beliefs.
- Causing questions as to the meaning of the death.

When death strikes a member of a school community, there will be a wide range in types and severity of grief responses. These responses may range from intense and debilitating for those who were closest to the deceased, to indifference or even what might be classified as inappropriate, cruel, or callous comments by those who did not know or did not like the person. Some callous comments do not reflect the person's true feelings but are caused by the shock, confusion, and fear caused by the death (Frantz, 1997).

It is not uncommon for a person who was not really close to the deceased to have an intense reaction. When this happens, it is often due to an earlier loss the person has experienced—a student whose grandparent died six months ago, a teacher who had a stillborn baby years before, or someone going through a divorce. Although many people feel that experiencing loss helps to handle subsequent loss more easily, it can also have the reverse effect. The pain of old losses can be brought to the surface and compound the response to this new loss.

☐ Anticipatory Grief

It is also normal for an individual who is anticipating the upcoming death of someone to experience normal grief responses, as if the death has already occurred. This is known as anticipatory grief and can be experienced by all age groups. At first glance, one might think that anticipatory grief is a negative response because of the pain it causes. Although this fact cannot be denied, anticipatory grief helps a grieving individual in the following ways:

- Acknowledging the reality of the death gradually over time
- Becoming sensitized (to some degree) to the death by mentally rehearsing the death
- Having the opportunity to tie up unfinished business with the dying person
- Being able to say goodbye

One should not believe the myth that if you mourn before a person dies, you will not mourn after the death. Anticipated loss is no less painful than unanticipated loss; however, the preparation of anticipatory grief allows for less of an assault on the mourners' adaptive capacities.

Rosen (1990) writes that the process of anticipatory grief contains an intrinsic paradox: simultaneously holding on to and letting go of the dying person. Nevertheless, even the death of a young person will have a dramatically different effect on people if it is anticipated. Along with previously mentioned benefits, having time to prepare allows some people to feel they have had some impact on the dying person.

Morgan (1993) believes that because grieving actually begins before the dying person dies, there is opportunity for preventive or therapeutic interventions before the death, which can sometimes facilitate grief work and a more positive post-death bereavement for the survivors.

☐ Grief in Schools

Holland (1993) reported that 70% of primary schools studied had bereaved children and many of these presented physical or psychological problems. In 40% of these school children, the following disruptive behaviors were evident:

- Violence
- Anger
- Crying
- Withdrawal
- Insecurity
- Overattachment
- Obsessive behavior
- Depression
- Lack of concentration
- Deterioration in school work

People who deny their grief, pretend it's not a big deal, insist they're not going to let it bother them, or try to cover it up with bravado, laughter, or stoicism, usually have a much harder time resolving their grief than do people who are able to grieve more expressively.

Holland & Ludford (1995) state that their research of secondary school students suggests that although these students are likely to have a more sophisticated concept of death, in practice they may lack sympathetic support in schools with a large number of students. Eighty-seven percent of schools which replied to the authors' questionnaire reported post-bereavement psychological or physical problems such as:

- Anger
- Depression
- Withdrawal
- Attention-seeking behavior
- Reduced levels of motivation
- Lack of concentration
- Increased absenteeism

In her book, *Life and Loss: A Guide to Helping Children*, Goldman (1994) lists the following feelings, thoughts and behaviors of the grieving child:

- Child retells events of the deceased's death and funeral
- Child dreams of the deceased
- Child feels the deceased is with him or her in some way
- Child rejects old friends and seeks new friends who have experienced a similar loss
- Child wants to call home during the school day
- Child can't concentrate on homework or class work
- Child bursts into tears in the middle of class
- Child seeks medical information on death of deceased
- Child worries excessively about his or her own health
- Child sometimes appears to be unfeeling about loss
- Child becomes the "class clown" to get attention
- Child is overly concerned with caretaking needs

Accordingly, a wide range of grief behaviors need to be tolerated. These include screaming in anguish; pounding the lockers in anger; sobbing in the hallway; stunned silence; an inability to answer even simple questions; seeming totally unaffected as if nothing happened; or stating, as one boy did upon being told of his friend's suicide, "Good, now I don't have to pay him the ten bucks I owe him." This last remark was made in shock, and the boy spent the next month being verbally attacked and apologizing over and over for it (Frantz, 1990).

Factors Affecting Grief

Contrary to what most adults think, studies have shown that children do think about death. A child's, adolescent's, or adult's belief structure surrounding death and how he responds when a death occurs, is determined by a number of different factors. These factors may involve the grieving person, the deceased, and the facts surrounding the death itself.

☐ The Grieving Person

Our personalities develop through a combination of genetics and the dynamics of our own environment. These external manifestations of our internal view of life are a major part of what differentiates us from others— what creates our image or individuality. This view of events and their consequences has an effect on our response to death. This does not mean that a person with an upbeat, positive, and joyful personality will not experience the pain of grief. It may mean, however, that the strength of that personality can allow the griever to recover in a normal progression. Conversely, a person with the opposite type of personality may have a more difficult time adjusting because he does not have the strength of a positive personality to fall back on during a crisis.

Normal Coping Behavior

Most people behave in a similar way when confronted with different stressors in their lives. If someone becomes physically ill, cries, becomes angry, or turns inward with silence and introspection when under stress, that is usually how he will respond to a death of a significant person in his life. That is why it is important for those counseling the grieving to know about past coping behaviors. The uninformed caregiver might interpret the behavior of a person who does not cry as uncaring or cold, when in reality this is normal coping behavior for that individual.

Number of Previous Losses and Deaths

One of the troublesome aspects of grief is that it can be cumulative. This means that a person does not always gain strength from each loss he experiences. It's true that someone can gain knowledge about the effect of loss and his response to it each time he experiences a new loss. This doesn't mean, however, that each loss makes the next one's adjustment easier. In fact, just the opposite usually occurs: The negative effects build up and are brought to the surface during subsequent losses.

Grief overload can also be a factor. Simply stated, this means that a person can experience too many losses in his life, and the losses do not need to be the same. The student who, in a two-year period, experiences the death of a friend, the divorce of parents, a move to a new home and school, and the disappearance of a pet is a prime candidate for grief overload. This overload often manifests itself in what others consider an exaggerated response to the most recent loss.

Concurrent Stressors

Just as a person can experience grief overload from previous losses, he can also experience a stress overload from stressful events that occur at the same time. A teacher who experiences the death of one of her students while she is also going through a divorce, dealing with a rebellious adolescent daughter, and facing financial difficulties may not be able to react with her usual "together" response.

Expectations of Local, Cultural, and Religious Groups

As stated previously, grief is an individual response—everyone responds differently. However, part of our response is determined by what is expected of us by members of important groups in our lives. Part of a person's behavior can be dictated and nurtured by important affiliations in his life.

These dictates can become so ingrained in our psyches that we are not even aware of their source. It is natural for us to respond that way, so we do it. In times of crisis, we often revert to what seems instinctual.

If the emphasis on multicultural diversity in our schools over the last decade has taught us anything, it is that what is right and appropriate for one group of people may not be the same for another group. A public outburst of emotion and crying at the funeral in one ethnic group might be seen as totally unacceptable to a different ethnic group.

Available Support Network

Experience and research in thanatology, the study of death, has shown repeatedly that the more positive support a griever has, the easier he will recover or adjust to a death. This support can come from family, friends, co-workers, or in the case of a student, school. This is one of the reasons that school can be so important to students and staff who are experiencing a loss. School supplies so much support in so many areas, it is a natural environment in which to seek help with grief.

Gender Conditioning

As much as the world is trying to prevent and remove gender stereotyping, in reality it is still quite prevalent. In no area is it more obvious than in society's expectations for how one should grieve. Men (boys) are still expected to be stronger than women (girls) are. Boys are encouraged to be strong. Wiseman (1998) explains that men have been conditioned to express anger more than grief or fear. Consequently, their grief is more likely to express itself in an angry form. Women have been taught that sadness is a safer emotion than anger, and they may end up crying when, in fact, they are more angry than sad.

Physical and Mental Health

The fact that grief can contribute to ill health, both physically and mentally, makes the state of health of an individual at the time of a death an important factor in determining the outcome of the experience. Good health does not guarantee a person an easy experience. It does, however, give the griever one more positive defense mechanism to help him in his task.

Pre-Death Adjustment Time

Having time to prepare for a death has both positive and negative outcomes for an individual. The ability and opportunity to tell the dying person things you want him to know can be a very positive experience. Having the time to say "Goodbye," "I love you," "You are my best friend," or "I will miss you" can be meaningful to both the dying person and the bereaved survivor. On the other hand, having to watch a person slowly degenerate from the healthy person he once was into a sickly specter of his former self can be heartbreaking.

The grief one experiences during this pre-death time is known as anticipatory grief. It is the pain experienced from anticipating the person's death, what life will be without that person, how the actual death will occur, and how the dying person actually feels about dying. Experiencing these feelings before the death can help relieve some of the grief following the death. (See additional information under Anticipatory Grief in Chapter 1).

Unfinished Business with the Deceased

One of the most common phrases people use after someone dies, especially in the case of a sudden death, is "If only I had a little more time." Most of us go through our lives with some loose ends hanging in our relationships. We don't always let people know how much they mean to us. Arguments or ill-feelings are left unattended with the intention of straightening things out later. The more of this unfinished business that remains after a death, the more difficult the adjustment can be.

Secondary Losses

When someone important to us dies, when we lose a job, or our marriage breaks up, it is considered a primary loss in our lives. Along with most primary losses, there are accompanying secondary losses. A secondary loss is one that comes about because of a primary loss.

Secondary losses often involve the loss of some type of status. When a student's best friend dies, the surviving student is no longer a best friend. When a marriage breaks up, the two individuals are no longer a husband and a wife, and it may mean the loss of a comfortable daily routine. When one's brother dies, the survivor is no longer a sibling. In some instances, the secondary losses involve more concrete circumstances, such as the loss of the family "bread winner," which can mean not being able to afford tuition, necessitating a transfer to a different school, or moving to different locale. The secondary loss can also be something more abstract such as the loss of the dreams and expectations a parent has for a child's future.

☐ The Deceased

Importance of the Relationship

One misconception in our society is that the closest relationships we have are with family members. In many instances, this is not the case. Students' relationships, especially the relationships with special peers, can be the strongest ones they have. The special relationship that can develop between a student and a teacher can be the most important and positive relationship in a student's life. For some, grandparents are a strong source of support and inspiration. The deaths of these people can be overwhelming.

The psychological intensity of the pre-death relationship between the deceased and the mourner will influence the mourner's response. The grief reaction will often increase or decrease in severity relative to the intensity of the relationship (Rando, 1984). The closer the relationship, the more intense the response.

There is more to determining the nature of a relationship than by looking at the family dynamics of how someone is related to another person. We must look at the quality of the relationship in emotional terms. Cook and Oltjenbruns (1989) explain, "The death of someone who was regarded as an intimate, a confidant, and a major source of support has a much greater impact than the death of someone who may have spent much time with the survivor but was never emotionally close" (p. 60).

It becomes clear when considering relationships that the death of a friend may cause a more severe response than the death of a family member. In a school community, close emotional relationships are common among students. There are also close emotional ties between some teachers and students. A death in a school has the potential to have a major impact on the response of students and staff.

Personal Qualities

Each of us has personal qualities that endear us to others. Likewise, we often have qualities that can be aggravating, annoying, troublesome, and upsetting. When someone dies, there are usually aspects of that person we will miss and others we won't miss. It's human nature to like fun-loving, caring, and supportive people and to dislike bullies, antagonists, mean-spirited, and negative people. This is especially true for young people.

Age of Deceased

Almost everyone feels that the death of a child or adolescent is the most tragic. We expect to follow the normal course of nature—the young survive and the old die. One exception is the death of a newborn. Many people feel there should be less grief when a newborn dies because they believe there was too short a time for much love and bonding to take place.

Fulfillment of Dreams

One of the reasons we feel that the death of young people is so tragic is because they have not lived to fulfill their dreams, experience the wonders of life, and feel a sense of accomplishment. This can also be felt about adults who we feel never accomplished their goals. With a child, we feel more as if he was cheated of the opportunity rather than the opportunity having passed him by.

☐ The Death

Adjusting to any death is difficult enough for most people. Individuals experiencing a death attributed to traumatic cause such as an accident, murder, or suicide face a compounded grief period. Grief is often intensified, since there is little or no opportunity to prepare for the loss, say goodbye or complete unfinished business. In addition, the nature of the loss can bring on grief reactions such as anger, guilt, and hopelessness, among others. There can also be a lingering sense of disorganization and consuming obsession with the person who died (Doka, 1996).

Accident

Feelings of guilt may be exaggerated in survivors if they believe they had some personal responsibility in not having been able to prevent the accident. Survivors may feel they contributed to the death by something they did or did not do, such as preventing someone from driving when he had been drinking. The blame is not always personal and could be directed at others. Although no one is ever fully prepared for the death of someone he cares about, when the death is anticipated there is an opportunity for some degree of closure. In sudden and violent death, however, there is no time to prepare. The survivor's ability to even understand what has happened is severely impaired. It is difficult, if not impossible, to begin the work of mourning a loss before understanding the nature and the enormity of what has happened (Froggie, 1992).

The suddenness and violence of an unexpected accident will usually compound the severity of survivors' grief. Lord (1996) believes that in most cases of vehicular crashes, family members say goodbye on a very normal day, in a very normal way, fully expecting their loved one to return at a designated time. Instead, several hours after his or her expected arrival time, a police officer knocks on the door, bringing the family the worst news of their lifetime. Or even worse, the unexpected message comes by phone. None of this is to say that one kind of traumatic loss is worse than another. Whatever happens to the members of a given family is the worst for them. But having no psychological preparation is different from having some warning.

Along with the normal reaction to death, people whose loved one experienced a violent, unexpected death also experience feelings of senselessness, fear, powerlessness, and unreality. The traumatic nature of the death can cause physical disfigurement to the body of the deceased, causing some families to choose a funeral service that does not involve viewing of the deceased person. They mistakenly feel that it would be easier on everyone, or in the case of a suicide, more appropriate, to have a closed casket.

In reality, the survivors of a tragic death are probably the ones who need to view the body more than if the death was due to a lingering illness. Seeing is believing. It helps to combat some of the denial that takes place. Often, seeing the body after the funeral director has prepared it relieves some of the survivor's anguish brought on by the mutilation or disfigurement of the body.

Homicide

One of the most difficult deaths to cope with is a homicide. When a teacher, student, or other member of the school's community is robbed of his or her life through the act of murder, survivors are left with a profound sense of shock, rage, helplessness, and vulnerability. Close friends and family of the victim are often inflicted with devastating emotional trauma.

Reactions to the grief process may be exacerbated due to the violent nature of the homicide. This is almost a certainty if the survivor actually witnesses the crime, as Frank Wade did when he watched the young killers shoot another student in the back in Littleton, Colorado. Dr. Spencer Eth did a study of 52 children who had witnessed the murder of a parent. Eth found that these children suffered severe emotional and learning problems including depression, short attention spans, violent behavior, nightmares, and memory loss (Doherty, 1989).

In 1998, in Niagara Falls, New York, Sean Gutschall died after being beaten on his way home from school. Other students were in a state of shock to think that something as common as an after-school fight could end in the murder of one of their peers. One student told the author, "Things like this just don't happen here."

The anger of normal grief is also intensified and directed at the murderer, the police, or the court system. The survivors may experience the tribulations of the criminal justice system, including delays, the perceived injustice of bail, the lack of legal standing for the victim's family, their inability to respond to counter charges and possible second trials, short sentences, and even acquittals (Doka, 1994). This anger can lead to a preoccupation with thoughts of revenge, especially if the murderer is not punished severely enough in the survivors' judgment.

Survivors can also be preoccupied with and distressed by thoughts of any suffering the victim may have experienced. They are often terrorized by fears for their own safety and think that they cannot carry on a normal life. People often don't know what to say to survivors, so they avoid them, causing feelings of loneliness and desertion.

The mind is overloaded with the events prior to, during, and after the murder. There is a constant dwelling on the events: what happened, when, how, where, who did what, and the often unanswerable, *why*? There may be questions that have been answered in a logical sequence by law enforcement officers, victim advocates, and other officials. None of the answers are *good enough*. The mind is searching to understand something that is incomprehensible. The act of reordering the events in order to understand them takes much longer than we may expect. This cognitive dissonance may continue for months or years, and may be triggered in the form of a delayed grief reaction by court proceedings or other events relating to the murder for years (Redmond, 1989).

As with accidental death, guilt plagues some survivors of a murder victim if they feel they could have prevented the murder. The author interviewed Daryl, a 16-year-old boy who was one of four students who survived a drive-by shooting. His feeling of happiness at not being shot was countered by guilt for not pulling his friend, who was shot, out of the way. He reflected, "If only I had thought faster, I could have saved him."

Among the most difficult emotional reactions to understand by survivors, family members, friends, therapists, and others who serve the victimized survivors are the intensity, duration, and frequency of anger and rage. For the homicide survivor, the rage and desire to violently destroy the murderer of the loved one compounds the normal anger of grief. The psyche is dominated by images of what the survivors *would, could,* and *should* do to the murderer. Elaborate plans of torturous treatment may be devised. The images of seeing the murderer suffer in a more horrendous manner than that in which one's own loved one suffered are normal reactions for the murder victim's survivors (Redmond, 1990).

Suicide

Suicide ranks as the leading cause of non-accidental death among people aged 15 to 24 years. Most survivors say that their grief after a suicide was complicated by severe feelings of guilt. They are haunted with thoughts such as, "Why didn't I see it coming?" "How could I not have known?" "Did I miss a warning signal?" and "Why didn't he come to me?"

There is also considerable anger after a suicide, often directed at the deceased. Survivors feel punished, hurt, deceived, and frightened, and ask, "How could he do this to me?" Suicide is not supposed to happen; it is not in the natural order of life. This anger at the deceased, in turn, causes guilt, as loved ones question their anger at the person who committed suicide.

For those of us who would not choose an intentional death, it is unthinkable that someone among our friends or family would. It creates so many unanswered questions, leaves so much unknown, and thus fuels fear. Survivors fear for their own safety, irrationally thinking, "If he could be driven to suicide, anyone could, including me." They also fear that others may imitate the act and fear that nothing in their life is certain. A suicide can threaten our basic beliefs about how the world is and leave us feeling unsure, insecure, unsafe, and wondering what we can count on with certainty (Frantz, 1990).

Prolonged Illness

Most of this chapter has discussed violent, unexpected deaths. There are, of course, deaths that are expected, with the actual dying period being prolonged. As mentioned earlier in this book, prolonged illness gives people the opportunity to complete any unfinished business with the dying person. It does, however, cause people to experience anticipatory grief. With students, this dying interval can mean a drop in grades, acting out, loss of interest, lack of concentration, or even aggressiveness and anger.

Acceptability of the Death

As stated earlier, grief can be caused by different loss situations. Some of these situations are given little attention due to society's lack of recognition of the particular loss. Not all deaths are accepted equally by society. Doka (1989) first labeled the phenomenon as disenfranchised grief, grief that is not openly acknowledged, publicly mourned, or socially supported.

Common examples are relatives and friends of criminals who are sent to prison or who were killed while committing a crime, abusive parents or spouses, or those with AIDS. One such situation that has occurred with certain types of violent events in schools revolves around the issue of individuals who were friends of the person who committed the violent act. A person who is grieving a loss that is not recognized by society will usually have a more difficult time adjusting to the loss. Aside from not having anyone who is empathetic and understanding to talk with, the griever begins to question the "rightness" or "wrongness" of his grief— "What type of person am I that would grieve for a murderer?" or "What's wrong with me? No one else feels this way."

A son, a grandchild, or husband does something terrible and the family name is tainted forever. While the family of the dead grieve and are comforted, the family of the accused and convicted also suffer. For the rest of their lives, they live with the deed, the stigma, and, only occasionally, the sympathy of strangers (Feinsilber, 1998).

The appearance to the griever that his grief is inappropriate can lead to his hiding external responses and ignoring his internal feelings. This combination can lead to a condition known as abnormal or pathologic grief, which could develop into physical or emotional problems at a later time.

Children's Reaction to Death

The most common mistake adults make when communicating with children who are grieving is assuming that children think like adults. In doing so, grieving adults frequently project their own fears and perceptions of death onto the children with whom they are dealing. The effect of this type of projection is that children miss an opportunity to learn to face loss in a manner appropriate to their developmental age, if not the opportunity to confront the loss altogether (Giblin & Ryan, 1991).

Chronological age is one way of classifying a child's understanding of death. Children appear to proceed from little or no understanding of death to recognition of the concept in the realistic form. While stages are most often listed in chronological order, the individual child may deviate from the specific age range and the particular behavior associated with it. While evidence does appear for the age-level understanding of children's concepts of death, one needs to keep in mind that development involves much more than simply growing older. Environmental support, behavior, attitudes, responsiveness of adults, self-concept, intelligence, previous experiences with death, and a number of other factors play an important role in the individual child's understanding of death (Wolfelt, 1983).

☐ Birth to Two Years

It is hard to assess how much infants grieve. We do know that they react with distress to the loss of the primary caregiver (usually the mother). In

17

addition, they may be able to sense the distress of those around them when it takes the form of crying, changes in schedules and routines, and additional noise and stimuli in the home environment. The absence of smiling faces, periods of play, and being held may have a cumulative effect. Infants may become cranky, cry often for no apparent reason, and alter their eating and/or sleeping patterns (Kroen, 1996).

If separation continues, the child manifests despair and sadness. If separation continues over a long period of time, the child will eventually become detached from everyone unless a constant, caring person takes over. During this stage, if the loss is someone other than the mother, such as a father or sibling, it is difficult to tell whether the child's reaction is truly a reaction to the loss itself or if the child is simply mirroring the grief of the mother (Newton, 1990).

Summary of Reactions for Children from Birth to Two Years

- Do not understand finality of death
- Can miss the presence of primary caregiver
- Will react to loss by crying, altering eating/sleeping schedules
- Can become detached

☐ Two to Five Years

At this age, the young child has developed the capacity to think, reflect, inquire, and affect a degree of self-control. This gives him a greater degree of independence and an enhanced sense of self-esteem. Experiencing a death at this age undermines children's self-confidence, and their world becomes unreliable and insecure (Pennells & Smith, 1995). They cry, yearn, and become clingy, and in play, they will often make attempts at reunion with the deceased person.

Children in this age group see death as temporary and reversible. They have little understanding of time. A day, a week, a year, or forever can all seem the same. A child can miss a person who is gone and is very aware of non-verbal communication such as changes in his personal family routine or in the moods of others.

Frequently, young children are concerned about the physical well-being of the deceased, wondering how he will keep warm and get food after burial (Bertois & Allen, 1988). They are not yet capable of cognitive reciprocity. They cannot learn outside the realm of their own experiences. Four- or five-year-olds can be quite interested in dead things and may want to see and touch the deceased.

It is not unusual for children of this age group to repeatedly ask the same questions about the deceased such as, "Will Billy be at school tomorrow?" Although this can be frustrating to an adult, children get reassurance from hearing the same answer over and over. Many don't know how they should act, so they confront visitors or strangers with statements like, "My daddy died" in order to pick up clues on how to respond or react (Overbeck & Overbeck, 1992). At times they may act as if the death never happened, while at other times they may react in a regressive manner. These are all normal reactions.

Summary of Reactions for Children Ages Two to Five

- Do not understand finality of death
- Believe death is reversible
- Do not always have vocabulary to express grief
- Feelings may be acted out in behavior and play
- Have an interest in dead things
- May ask some questions over and over
- React in light of their own experiences with death

☐ Six to Nine Years

Children in this age group have a much greater ability to understand death and its consequence than do younger children. Although they may cling to some of their fantasies, they are able to grasp the reality and, more importantly, the finality of death. However, this does not mean that they are ready to accept death or respond to it rationally (Kroen, 1996). To them, death only takes other people. Death is personified in the forms of monsters, ghosts, or other frightening creatures. This fantasy allows the child to be able to hide or run away from it, thereby keeping him safe.

Another characteristic of this age group that can be particularly troublesome for them is their tendency to engage in magical thinking. Children of this age will often think or wish "bad" things to happen to other people. If a person to whom they wished harm should die, this magical thinking can make them feel that they caused the death. Children feel responsible for what happens in the world around them (Goldman, 1994).

Their lack of vocabulary to express how they feel is one of the reasons they act out these feelings in their behavior. Children at this age have strong feelings of loss, but they also have extreme difficulty expressing it. Crying, withdrawal, frightening dreams, aggressiveness, and misbehavior are common. They often need permission to grieve. Boys have particular difficulty with this and frequently exhibit aggressive responses and play patterns (Rando, 1988).

Summary of Reactions for Children Ages Six to Nine

- Beginning to understand finality of death
- Believe death only happens to others
- Death is personified as ghosts or monsters
- Engage in magical thinking, and may feel they caused death
- Have strong feelings of loss
- May lack vocabulary to express feelings
- Often need permission to grieve, especially boys

☐ Nine to Twelve Years (Pre-Adolescence)

Children of this age group can understand that death is final and irreversible. Normally, these children have short attention spans. It is typical for them to cry and feel depressed one minute and then play as if nothing happened the next. This behavior becomes an issue for a child in this age group when adults interpret it as if the child is not upset over the loss. Statements like, "How can you behave like that with your mother lying in her grave?" can intensify a child's feelings of guilt and low self-worth.

Egocentric concerns, such as who will take care of them or whom they will play with are common in children of this age group. Although their vocabulary is advanced enough to express their feelings, they may not talk about what is bothering them. Instead, sadness and anger will build up inside them and manifest themselves in behavior problems. School is a primary environment for these children, so it is realistic to expect misbehavior, lack of concentration, and a drop in grades.

Overbeck and Overbeck (1992) agree that allowing and encouraging children to express their feelings will help. They write, "Children at this age must be encouraged over and over again to talk about the loss and express their deep inner feelings in order to allow mourning to result in a positive outcome" (p. 52).

There is an interest and curiosity in the physical aspects of death and what happens after death. Children in this age group may identify with the deceased and imitate their mannerisms. Boys in this age group are more aggressive in acting out their feelings.

Summary of Reactions of Children Ages Nine to Twelve

- Understand finality of death
- Have curiosity about the physical aspects of death

- Have vocabulary to express feelings, but often choose not to
- Need encouragement to express feelings
- May identify with deceased by imitating mannerisms
- May have short attention spans

☐ Thirteen to Eighteen Years (Adolescence)

Adolescents understand the meaning of death much as do adults. They realize that it is irreversible and that it happens to everyone. The intensity of grief for adolescents is described by Glass (1990): "Losses such as death affect the total life of the high school students involved, their work at school, their part-time jobs, their leisure activities, their relationship with friends and family, and their concepts about themselves" (p. 155).

Normally developing adolescents can think about death in an abstract, conceptual, formal, mature, scientific, or adult way. This fact on its own does not necessarily mean that they actually or even frequently do think about death in those ways. To have the ability to think in a certain way is not the same as actually thinking in that way. It may be especially difficult for these youngsters to think of death as something that will eventually happen to them (Grollman, 1995).

Of all the age groups, adolescents appear to have the most difficult time dealing with death and dying. Unlike younger children, teenagers have the additional problems of frustration, anxiety, and confusion of normal puberty, which intensifies their grief. Death adds to their already conflicting feelings of unattractiveness, insecurity, not belonging, and not being in control of self and surroundings. Grief reactions can be influenced by peer pressure more in this age group than in others.

At a time when adolescents need to be comforted and supported, they are often put in the position of being the protector, comforter, and caregiver (Morgan, 1990). Statements such as "We need you to be strong" make some adolescents feel they must be a comfort to others. By keeping their own emotions suppressed, they give the outward appearance that they are handling things well, while on the inside they are falling apart.

Adolescents philosophize about death and search for its meaning. They also experience conflicting feelings about death. They may feel as if they are immune to death, while experiencing at the same time anxiety and fear over their own death. Some adolescents deal with this fear by engaging in activities that can threaten their lives, such as abusing drugs and alcohol or unsafe driving.

Academic achievement and competition are also a part of the bereaved teen's world. While they are trying to survive the death of someone in their lives, pressure to get good grades or get into the right college still exists. Struggling with a death often makes it difficult for adolescents to perceive the value others place on academics (Wolfelt, 1991).

Adolescent males and females have different responses to death. Male adolescents often exhibit anger and aggression, whereas female adolescents seem to need comforting, reassurance and physical closeness.

Summary of Reactions of Adolescents Ages 13 to 18

- Have an adult understanding of death
- Can express feelings, but often choose not to
- Philosophize about life and death
- Search for meaning of death
- Death affects entire life—school, home, relationships
- May appear to be coping well when they are not
- Are often thrust into role of comforter
- Participate in dangerous behavior like drugs and alcohol

☐ Additional Reactions

Goldman (1994) advises teachers of any grade to be aware that the bereaved child may:

- Become the class clown
- Become withdrawn and unsociable
- Wet his bed or have nightmares
- Become restless in staying seated
- Call out of turn
- Not complete schoolwork
- Have problems listening and staying on task
- Become overly talkative
- Become disorganized
- Show reckless physical action
- Show poor concentration around external stimuli
- Show difficulty in following directions

The following warning signs identified by Morgan (1994) may also be exhibited by grieving students:

- Inability to concentrate
- Chronic absenteeism
- Poor grades and/or neglect of homework
- Poor scores on standardized tests not related to intelligence quotient or learning disabilities

- Uncooperative and quarrelsome behavior
- Sudden behavior changes
- Shy and withdrawn demeanor
- Compulsive behaviors
- Chronic health problems
- Signs of neglect and abuse
- Low self-esteem
- Anger, anxiety, and/or depression
- Poor coping skills
- Unnecessary fearfulness
- Difficulty adjusting to change

Response Planning Procedures

When the school community experiences a death, it is as though someone has dropped a monkey wrench into the machinery and everything comes to a standstill. One quickly finds that getting on with the business of the day is difficult at best (Cassini & Rogers, 1991). Many staff members and students are too upset to fulfill their responsibilities for a day or two. The main office can be flooded with phone calls from parents, the media, and other interested officials or residents.

People need direction, structure, and support at this time. Schools should therefore have a plan that can be readily implemented. The plan must permit prompt intervention geared toward reestablishing stability, providing support, and facilitating the needs of students, staff, and the community.

As logical as planning ahead for a crisis may seem, it is not always an easy process. The literature has identified certain obstacles that can interfere and even derail crisis planning and implementation. Lichtenstein (1997) suggests that administrators may be conditioned to remain quiet regarding any kind of school commotion so as not to generate negative attention or blame. They may revert to an autocratic management style because of feeling singularly responsible.

McIntyre and Reid (1989) discuss the myth that taking action will make a crisis worse. Territorial issues exist about whose job it is to implement crisis planning, as it is usually not listed on anyone's job description. Oates (1988) believes the most common reaction to a crisis is to ignore it out of a fear that a response will worsen the situation and result in the criticism of an administrator.

The following steps for creating a school-level crisis response plan are adapted from the tasks developed by Frantz (1990), Pitcher and Poland (1992), and Sinkkonen (1989). They are designed to be effective, with minimum modification, for any grade level from elementary to high school.

☐ The Crisis Response Team

The beginning of any crisis response planning involves the creation of a Crisis Response Team. The object of such a team is to provide a group of trained volunteers who will be responsible for developing and implementing a response following the death of a student or staff member. Kline et al. (1995) and Lichtenstein et al. (1994) describe three types of crisis teams:

- Regional
- District
- School

Regional-level team.   This team is composed of representatives from district-level teams and professionals outside the school system. The purposes of this team are:

- Sharing of expertise and resources across the school district boundaries
- Coordinating response to a large-scale disaster such as a hurricane or tornado

District-level team.   This team includes administrators and other individuals, both inside and outside the school, who have special responsibility for and/or expertise in crisis response. The duties of this team include:

- Establishing district-wide guidelines and adapting recommendations of the regional team to district policies
- Enabling district staff to receive adequate, ongoing training
- Ensuring that each school has a fully operational crisis intervention team
- Serving as a liaison between the regional team and the individual school crisis teams
- Coordinating special assignments of school and community personnel in the event of a crisis
- Facilitating the sharing of staff and resources among schools
- Coordinating district-wide response when crisis involves more than one school
- Assisting school teams as necessary

School-level team.   This team serves as the heart of a response to a crisis. Staff members from individual schools are the most appropriate people to provide support assistance and long-term follow-up in their schools. According to Kline et al. (1995), the purposes of school crisis teams are to:

- Identify crisis team members in individual schools
- Train school crisis team members in crisis and related issues
- Convene school crisis teams to review school district procedures and to assign responsibilities
- Develop written school crisis plans
- Compile crisis information packets and assemble emergency supplies

The importance of the Crisis Response Team cannot be overemphasized. From the moment the team is called into action until the post-crisis evaluation, team members are part of a very important healing process. By performing its duties and fulfilling its responsibilities, the team will be helping the students and staff by reducing the fear and anxiety that accompanies the death of a student or staff member, educating them about the dynamics of grief, and preparing them for what they might experience.

☐ Creating a Crisis Response Plan

The recommended number of people on the Crisis Response Team varies. Poland and Pitcher (1990) recommend four to eight members, others recommend one for every 100 students or no more than 10 people on a team. At the least, it should consist of a representative from teaching faculty, counseling, administration, nursing, maintenance, transportation, and an outside consultant. The team should be empowered with the authority to make decisions during the crisis. Once the administration has recruited the volunteers to serve as a crisis response team, the team then becomes responsible for carrying out the remaining steps.

☐ Recruiting an Outside Consultant

An outside consultant with experience in dealing with deaths in a school should be recruited for the team. This is advisable even if you have qualified people on your staff. When death strikes, it may affect school professionals, rendering them incapable of taking on an advisory role. You need someone who is objective and not personally involved. Four groups of outside consultants should be considered by a Crisis Response Team to be valuable resources for a school during a crisis. These groups are:

- Grief specialists
- Mental health professionals
- Clergy
- Funeral directors

(See Chapter 5 for a description of the duties of each of these professionals.)

☐ Designating a Media Liaison

The Media Liaison will be the only person within the school or school district who will make statements to the press, radio, or television. This person will also be responsible for preparing and updating the news releases that will act as the only source of information coming from the school. All staff should be instructed not to speak to the media but to refer them to the liaison instead.

The individual chosen should be someone who is comfortable with appearing on television and radio. Because he will be responsible for all written communication to the media, he must have good written communication skills. This person should have a familiarity with school and district policies (Pitcher & Poland, 1992). (See Chapter 5 for a description of the responsibilities of the Media Liaison.)

☐ Developing a Media Policy

If there is a sensational nature to the death, such as a suicide, accident, or homicide, the media will probably converge on the school. The Crisis Response Team must determine whether the media will have access to the grounds, building, and students. Experience has shown that at times the media can be disruptive and upsetting.

In communicating with the media, Bark (1989) emphasizes the importance of being honest. Jay (1989) advocates a cooperative approach. The media should feel comfortable in verifying information received outside of the school with the media liaison. Elliott (1989) suggests that a school respond quickly with information on the tragedy. The longer it takes for the school to respond, the easier it is for the media to obtain misinformation elsewhere. The Crisis Response Team should strive to consider the media as an ally.

☐ Designating a Family Liaison

One member of the school staff who has been affected by the death should be designated as the representative who will be the contact person for the family of the deceased. This person should be someone who is empathetic, a good communicator, and knowledgeable in the grieving process. He will make and maintain contact with the family of the deceased, obtain information the school needs, and supply any assistance the family needs from the school. (See Chapter 5 for a description of the Family Liaison's responsibilities.)

☐ Creating and Updating a Telephone Tree

It is vital that all staff members are notified when a death has occurred (especially if it is after school hours) and are given the time and location for the emergency staff meeting to be held before class begins the next day. Everyone must be made aware of the importance of contacting the person(s) who are of his or her responsibility. If someone fails to contact the next person, everyone else below him on the tree is also uninformed. Stevens (1990) states that most schools need a better communication system than they presently have for disseminating information to staff members. Keeping the phone tree accurate and up-to-date each semester is vital to ensuring all staff will be contacted.

☐ Developing a Staff-Sharing Policy

Often, when a death occurs, a school does not have enough "in-house" professionals available for meeting with upset students and staff. Arrangements can be made with counselors and other trained individuals from other schools, within or even from outside your district, to be available in an emergency.

☐ Developing a Arrangement with Non-School Professionals

Non-school professionals, such as counselors, psychologists, psychiatrists, social workers, clergy, funeral directors, and nurses can supplement your school's staff of trained professionals. A list of interested community resources should be created. These resources must be people who are trained in bereavement counseling and who are able to modify their own schedule to come to the school in an emergency. Depending on your budget, you can look for those requiring payment or for volunteers.

☐ Hiring Substitute Teachers

Some classroom teachers may be too upset to be able to function normally or help their students cope. An agreement should be made with your administration for calling in two or three substitute teachers. These may or may not be necessary, but as a precaution they should be called in for at least the first day of school following the crisis.

☐ Identifying a Crisis Headquarters

One area or room should be designated as the center for crisis activities. This room should have a phone and a reliable person staffing it at all times. All incoming calls regarding the death should be routed through this room. The person staffing the room should know how to reach critical individuals such as the principal, Crisis Team Leader, Media Liaison, and Family Liaison. He should have the names and phone numbers of the other school and community resource people. All information and questions about the death from within the school should also be dealt with from this room.

☐ Identifying Crisis Counseling and Quiet Rooms

There should be another room set aside as a counseling center for people who need to talk to a professional. A school or community professional should be available in the room at all times. Another room should be designated as a quiet room for people who want to be alone. This room should also be staffed at all times, ideally with a professional or at least a non-professional who could refer people to the counseling room when necessary.

☐ Determining an Information Flow Pattern

The information flow pattern should be planned for ahead of time. For example, how will staff be notified throughout the day about changing information? Will they be notified by phone, through flyers in their mailboxes, or by a messenger? Also, how will you advertise the location and hours for the Headquarters, Counseling, and Quiet Rooms? You will need to consider who will make the announcement of the death to the students. An effective method combines the more personal touch of the teacher informing the students in class first and then a public announcement by the principal from his office.

☐ Formulating a School Policy on Funeral Attendance

Some students and staff members will wish to attend visiting hours at the funeral home or the actual funeral. The time for the ceremonies may be during regular school hours. With regard to students, questions such as transportation, parental permission, and supervision must be considered. The issue of staff attendance must also be considered. How many teachers can be released from class to attend? How will you replace a large number of teachers physically and monetarily? Can special arrangements be made with the family and the funeral home to conduct a service for school members only at some time outside of the normal school hours?

☐ Formulating a Policy on School Remembrance Activities

Some schools conduct, either in addition to or in place of funeral services, a special remembrance activity at the school. This may be a general assembly, tree planting, dedication of part of the yearbook, dedication of a plaque, or lowering of the flag. The specifics of the policy do not have to be worked out ahead of time, but a general policy should be developed.

The activities may differ with each death. If a member of the band dies, a ceremony centering on the band might be appropriate. If someone who was a member of the biology club dies, the emphasis may be different. Students should also be allowed to have input in determining the type of activity. This is an excellent method of coping with grief and learning about life and death (Stevenson & Powers, 1987).

☐ Determining Student Input

The Crisis Response Team should consider whether it wants student input, as well as the role that students, such as peer counselors, will play during the crisis? A responsible and interested student can add some dynamics and viewpoints that may be overlooked by an all-staff team.

☐ Availability of Reading Material on Death

Books, articles, and brochures concerning death and grieving should be made available during the crisis. This can be coordinated with the librarian. The books and longer articles can be kept in the library, while the shorter articles and brochures can be placed in the counseling and quiet rooms. Check with your outside professionals about obtaining informational material.

☐ Drafting a Letter to Parents

Parents should be notified when a death has occurred, informed of the measures the school is taking, given information on student grief, and provided with a phone number in order to call the school for information or assistance, as well as the time and date of any planned parent/community meeting.

☐ Planning for a Parent/Community Meeting

This meeting should be held in the evening one or two days after the funeral. The principal and all Crisis Response Team members and crisis professionals should be present. Information as to what parents can expect during the children's grieving period should be discussed. Time should be allowed for questions, especially if the death was by suicide, homicide, or drug-related.

☐ Planning for Postvention Evaluation

Make plans to schedule a meeting of representatives from all groups involved in the crisis response two weeks after the funeral. Feedback should be solicited and suggestions on how to improve the entire response should be discussed.

☐ Identification and Referral of At-Risk Students

There are always students who will have a more difficult time adjusting to death than others. These students are considered "at-risk," and include best friends, siblings, boyfriend or girlfriend, and those who may not have been close to the deceased but who are depressed, under great stress, have experienced other losses, or those who have been suicidal in the past. Their teachers, coaches, counselors, or friends should identify these students to the Crisis Response Team. A trained staff member should then sensitively and privately contact these students, letting them know that someone cares and can provide support and help. If serious cause for concern is detected, the student's parents should be contacted.

The following is an outline of the behaviors to look for when assessing children for risk. When considering these behaviors, the clinician is looking for extremes, and should not identify an at-risk child with mild behavioral indicators. The following suggestions for identifying possible at-risk individuals, aside from those listed above, as well as helping strategies was obtained from the Federal Emergency Management Agency's publication, *School Intervention Following a Critical Incident* (1991).

☐ Signs of At-Risk Students

1. Withdrawn/Quiet
- Holds head down
- Lack of eye contact
- Look of hopelessness, defeat, and no "light in eyes"
- Social isolation

What to Do:
- Respect the child's need to be quiet
- Try to find "a way in"
- Consider cultural differences around eye contact
- Tell child it is difficult to hear him when his head is down
- Focus on hopefulness, power, and strength
- Ask another child to respond to isolated child

2. Overly Responsible/Parental
- Taking care of those around him
- Doesn't discuss own feelings/denial of feelings
- Straight A student who worries about Fs
- Latchkey children

What to Do:
- Give the child permission and encouragement to play
- Acknowledge caretaking abilities and ask what can be done for him (you probably won't get an answer, but it plants the seed)
- Identify feelings in group (and own or others' feelings)

3. Hyper
- Cannot focus or sit still
- Distinction between high energy and hyper

What to Do:
- Allow child to leave group briefly to run around track, do cartwheels, etc.
- Give task while in a group
- Child may have to be removed permanently from group and worked with individually

4. Edgy/Jumpy
- Quick to anger
- Hypervigilant about others' opinions of self
- Quick to cry, overly sensitive

What to Do:
- Reflect child's angry feelings, model verbalizing feelings
- Notice and acknowledge anxiety of others' reactions to self
- Reflect these feelings to group
- Allow tears to flow freely, then ask questions

5. Vying for Attention
- Raises hand at every question, may push it in therapist's face
- Constantly interrupts others
- Has name on classroom board for talking too much

What to Do:
- Acknowledge child's enthusiasm and your desire to hear from him
- Explain need to hear from others
- Stop interruptions in progress
- Acknowledge importance of child's input

6. Flat Affect
- Attitude of non-caring
- Little range in voice tone or volume

What to Do:
- Be animated, but not too excitable
- Speak in "animal" voices and ask child to do same
- Talk about how "other" people learn to not care

7. Out of Control Behavior
- Little or no respect for authority/limits
- Lashing out at others

What to Do:
- Set clear limits and realistic consequences
- Follow through with consequences
- Give child respect

☐ Crisis/Grief and Family Tree Files

The following two systems for tracking at-risk students have proven useful to the schools who have implemented them.

System #1: Since grief can affect students over a long period of time, and can affect behavior and grades, a file (to be updated by the students' teachers) will be kept in the office of students who experience tragedy or death.

1. Information will be put on a 3 x 5 index card. Please include:

Student's name _____ Grade ___ Date _____

Incident: Briefly describe the important information. _____

_____

_____

Teacher's Name _____

Family member to contact and phone number _____

---

2. It is the responsibility of the teacher to fill out a card when a situation arises, and for forwarding the information to the next grade level teacher and/or next building.

System #2:

Family Tree File

Dear Parents:

    Once in a while it is important that the school be made aware of family relationships within our building. This is especially true in case of an emergency or crisis that might effect siblings, cousins, etc. in our school. Often, these relations have different surnames, and we may be unaware of the relationship and, therefore, unable to provide needed support to our children.

    For this reason, we are establishing a Family Tree File for all three (3) school buildings. The information will be confidential and the file will be maintained in our office for use only in a serious situation.

Please complete the following information and return it to your child's teacher.

Sincerely,_____

— —

Name of Student:_____ Date of Birth:_____

Address:_____

Parents/Guardians:_____

Full Names of Siblings & Schools Attending:

_____

Full Names of Cousins or Other Close Relations & Schools:

_____

☐ Planning for First Morning Staff Meeting

The school day following the tragedy should begin with an emergency meeting of all school staff, teachers, custodians, nurses, counselors, administrators, substitute teachers, cafeteria workers, resource room volunteers, etc. The community resource people should also be included in this meeting. A half-hour to 45 minutes should be allowed for this meeting, which should take place before the normal start of the school day. The meeting has two purposes, the first handled by the building principal, the second by the crisis consultant.

The principal should begin the meeting by announcing what has happened, giving as much information as possible with regard to the death, funeral, and family wishes. Staff members will function best if they are well-informed. Staff questions should be answered, and the plan for the day should be specifically given. The community resource people, media and family liaison individuals, and Crisis Response Team members should be introduced. The locations of the Crisis Center and Counseling Room should be designated, and plans for the after-school staff meeting should be announced.

A member of the Crisis Response Team or the crisis consultant should then address the group on what to expect from and how to respond to students, what to say in the homeroom or first class, and the importance of paying attention to the staff members' feelings and reactions about the death (Frantz, 1990).

☐ Developing Suggestions for Classroom Activities

Information on what teachers can do in class to help their students should be developed and distributed to faculty at the first staff meeting during the crisis. This material can also be distributed to faculty in a setting such as in-service training before the need arises. During homeroom or the first class teachers can:

- Give students the pertinent information regarding the death
- Describe the schedule for the day
- Give the location of the crisis room
- Encourage discussion
- Answer questions
- Refer students who request help or those the teacher feels need help
- Reassure the students that there is help available

☐ Planning for First Day After-School Staff Meeting

At the close of the first school day following the death, a second meeting should be held for all school staff. The principal or the Crisis Response Team members may lead the meeting. The purpose is to review the day's events, attending to what went well and what didn't, identifying the at-risk students or staff and how to help them, making any needed adjustments in the postvention plan, enunciating continuing postvention plans, and allowing the staff to raise questions for the crisis consultant or Crisis Response Team.

☐ Organizing and Conducting In-Service Training for Staff

Preparation for handling deaths at school *before a tragedy happens* is essential. It is the only way to assure rapid and sensitive handling of deaths invading the psychological sanctity of schools. In-service training programs for staff on handling grief and loss should be elevated to necessity rather than choice (Harris & Lord, 1990).

Stevenson and Powers (1987) recognize that training programs on death, grief, and coping should be scheduled for faculty and staff. The committee should develop guidelines for these in-service programs. In writing on the value of such programs, Cunningham and Hare (1989) maintain that an in-service training program could include information on:

- Adult grief
- Childhood grief
- The dynamics of a death in a school community
- The crisis response plan
- Activities for working through the grief process

☐ Conducting a Post-Crisis Evaluation

Every disaster plan should have as a requirement the conducting of a post-crisis evaluation. It is only by analyzing the results of our efforts that we can improve them and ensure a more effective response in future crises. Each step of the plan that was activated should be analyzed individually and as part of the whole.

Perea and Morrison (1997) suggest that a successful evaluation should yield the following results:

- Insure response was expeditious and compassionate
- Provide feedback for future training
- Reveal ways to update the plan
- Justify the budget
- Positively effect services for crisis victims

The *Alberta Bereavement and Loss Manual* (1992) recommends that the evaluation examine and determine the following issues:

1. Was the plan effective? If not, why not?
2. Were the survivors' needs met effectively? Partially? Not at all? What were the problems? How can they be rectified?
3. Were there any areas where further planning would have been helpful? If so, what were they? How could these areas be improved and changes implemented?
4. Did the key participants know their roles and carry out their responsibilities effectively?
5. Was responsibility evenly distributed or were some participants too weighed down to be fully effective? How can responsibilities be redistributed?
6. Based on your experience, what other factors should be considered in modifying the plan?

Staff Responsibilities

Following a tragedy such as the death of a student or staff member, it is not unusual for staff members to be emotionally upset and find it difficult to organize and prioritize tasks that must be performed. This chapter discusses the roles of certain staff members during a tragedy.

☐ The Role of the Principal

The key to successfully coping with a school tragedy rests with the principal's leadership (Snyder, 1993). A crisis of major proportion calls for enlightened leadership: a take-charge manner combined with effective teamwork and delegation of vital operations (Lichtenstein et al., 1994). As the chief officer of the building, the principal is responsible for the implementation of the crisis response plan. Aside from putting the plan into motion, the attitude he presents about the importance of the plan and how sensitively it should be carried out can set the tone for the manner in which the entire school responds. The principal's active participation and leadership is necessary from the first step of receiving the notification of death to the end of the immediate crisis, when the effectiveness of the response plan is evaluated.

Because of the nature of those who seek to become principals, it is not unusual for the principal to feel an obligation to be the strong shoulder for everyone to lean on. This can be difficult if he is experiencing his own grief. He should take advantage of the support people who are involved in the plan to help him cope with the emotional strain he will be under.

The family of the deceased, someone in school, or the police will notify the principal about a death of a student or staff member. At times he will unfortunately learn of it by reading about it in the newspaper, hearing about it on the radio, or seeing a report on television. If the information does not come from the family of the deceased, it will be necessary to contact the family to verify the information he has received.

Once the information is verified, the principal should notify the school superintendent. During this conversation, the principal can update the superintendent about what will be taking place at the school. If it is necessary for the principal to obtain approval for any of his plans, this is the opportunity to request it.

The principal will then notify the designated person on the Crisis Response Team. A meeting should be scheduled between the team and the principal as soon as possible. The team should be updated on all the information the principal has received up to this point. If it is necessary for the team to obtain approval for any actions it will be taking, this can be accomplished at this meeting.

If the death is one that the media will most likely sensationalize, the principal and the Media Liaison should prepare a statement for the media, providing them with the known facts and the steps the school will be taking to respond to the needs of those in the school community. The statement should give the name of the Media Liaison and how to contact him. It should also include any procedures that the media will need to follow to gain access to the school grounds, if that is going to be permitted. The Media Liaison should be given the media information and should confer with the principal as to the procedures being implemented and how to deal with them.

It will also be necessary to prepare an announcement for the teachers to read in class informing the students about the death. This is necessary to ensure that everyone receives the same information. A statement to be given to those making telephone inquiries should also be prepared, as well as a statement to all staff members, even if a staff meeting will be held.

A general staff meeting should be held as soon as possible, either to inform the staff of the death or to update them on developments since the information was made public. The members of the Crisis Response Team should be present to support grieving faculty, inform them of what to expect, and familiarize them with the crisis plan and the upcoming steps to be taken.

The principal should notify other school principals in the district. At this time, if necessary, he may request help from counselors at other schools. The other principals should also be informed of what will be occurring at the school. The principal should also hire a few extra substitute teachers to be available should some of the regular faculty be too upset to continue in their classes.

Release time for faculty to attend the funeral must be considered, as well as whether or not the principal himself will attend. A sympathy note should be written to the family of the deceased.

Contacting the Family of the Deceased

One of the most difficult tasks a principal must carry out when a death has occurred is contacting the family of the deceased to verify information, express condolences, and notify the family of the school's response. When calling for the first time, the principal should identify himself, tell the family member why he is calling, and from whom he heard the information. He must try to be as delicate as possible in his approach. For example:

> "Mrs. Thomas, this is Bill Gray, the principal at Lee High School. I am calling because I have received some tragic news from _____. He/she said that Bill died today."

The principal should listen to the response, express his sympathy, and inform the person that he feels it would be helpful for the students and staff to receive some information about the death:

> "Mrs. Jones, please accept my personal sympathy and that of the school. There will be a lot of questions tomorrow from our students and staff. I would like to supply the teachers with information they can give to their classes. Would you feel comfortable talking with me for a few minutes?
>
> The most helpful information would be how (or why) Bill died, the time, and if anyone else was with him (in the case of an accident). If you have any information about the funeral at this time, I will include that also." (For a suicide, the family should be asked what they would like to be announced as the cause of death. If it is later published in the newspaper as a suicide, staff can affirm that this is what the family had told them originally.)

The principal should reassure them of his concern and explain the procedures the school will be taking:

> "Mrs. Jones, the staff of Lee High School will help you in any way we can. I would like to have _____ act as our contact person for you. Would that be all right? His telephone number is _____ if you would like to write it down. Also, if it is okay with you, _____ will call you tomorrow morning to see if he can help and to let you know about the steps that the school has instituted to help our staff and students with Bill's death."

If the principal is also the liaison with the family, the statements should be rephrased.

Responsibilities

* Receive notification of death
* Verify information
* Notify superintendent
* Notify Crisis Response Team and call meeting
* Notify Media Liaison
* Schedule special staff meeting
* Hire substitute teachers
* Prepare announcement to be read in classes
* Prepare telephone inquiry statement
* Attend special staff meetings
* Make announcement to school
* Prepare and send letter to parents,
* Notify other principals
* Grant release time for funeral attendance
* Condolence note to family
* Attend funeral, if desired

☐ The Role of Crisis Team Members

Kline et al. (1995) offer a comprehensive description of the duties of the Crisis Response Team Chairperson, Assistant Chairperson, Communications Coordinator, and Crowd Management Facilitator.

Crisis Response Team Chairperson: Responsible for chairing all meetings of the crisis team and overseeing the board and the specific functioning of the team and its members.

Crisis Response Team Assistant-Chairperson/Staff Notification Coordinator: Assists the Chairperson in all functions and substitutes in the event of the unavailability of the Chairperson. Establishes, coordinates, and initiates telephone tree to contact staff after hours.

Communications Coordinator: Responsible for conducting all direct in-house communication. Screens incoming calls and maintains a log of telephone calls related to the crisis. Assists the Staff Notification Coordinator and helps maintain an accurate telephone directory of community resources and district-level staff.

Crowd Management Facilitator: Responsible, in collaboration with local law enforcement and fire departments, for planning mechanisms for crowd management in the event of various potential crises. Directly supervises the movement of students and staff in the event such plans are initiated. A crowd control plan must include arrangements to cordon off areas with physical evidence, assemble students and faculty for presentation, and in the event of an actual threat to the physical safety of students, assure the safe and organized movement of students to minimize the risk of harm.

☐ The Role of the Family Liaison

The staff member designated as the Family Liaison has an important responsibility. The impressions the family receives from talking to this person will be the impression they have of the entire school's response to the death of their child. The Family Liaison should be able to communicate in a sensitive way.

The Family Liaison's first call to the family should be made the day after the principal has verified the information. This time period will give the school an opportunity to implement its crisis plan and will allow the family to recover from the immediate shock of the first 24 hours. By this time, the family may also have made funeral arrangements, and the school needs this information.

Often, when a parent loses a child through death, one of the emotions he experiences is a feeling of powerlessness. He feels as if he has lost control of his life. Many parents who have lost a child through death feel they were unable to fulfill the most basic task a parent has—keeping their child safe. When talking with bereaved parents, anything that can be done, even in the simplest form, to help them regain some feeling of control can be helpful. The following questions and comments are designed to restore some control in these parents' lives.

In the first contact, the Family Liaison should identify who he is, offer his own sympathy and that of the staff, and share any personal feelings he may have had about the deceased student that would be appropriate. For example:

> "Mrs. Black, this is Mary Phillips. I am a teacher at City Elementary School. I am also the school's Family Liaison, which simply means that I am the person who will be able to help you most quickly with questions you may have or things you need done. Please feel free to contact me with any questions or requests that you may have at any time.
>
> "On behalf of the staff, I would like you to know how sorry we are to hear of Carl's death. I personally enjoyed having him in class; he had a wonderful sense of humor."

After the parent responds, let her know why you are calling:

> "I am calling for a few reasons. First, I wanted to let you know what steps we'll be taking at the school to help everyone cope with Carl's death." (Then explain your procedures simply.)

"When Bill Gray, the principal, spoke with you yesterday, you had not made the funeral arrangements yet. Do you have any information about them at this time? A number of people at the school have been asking for this information."

(After the parent's response): "Would it be all right if an announcement was made in our school regarding the time of the funeral?"

(After the parent's response): "Would you mind if we attended the funeral as a group? The students will be coming to the visiting hours either on their own or with their parents.

"Mrs. Black, some of the students would like to write a poem about Carl and one member of the group would like to read it at the funeral. Would you permit them to do that?"

(After the parent's response): "Thank you, we'll contact the funeral director to arrange it. May I call you tomorrow morning to see how you are doing and give you an update on activities at the school?"

The deceased student's or staff member's locker or desk may contain items that the family might like to have. If the family does not request these, return them about a week after the funeral. A visit at this time will be appreciated. This may be a difficult visit. Seeing the person's belongings will probably cause tears and some pain, but it is a healing activity. If the family member is alone, stay with her while she goes through the belongings so that she has someone with whom to share her feelings. It is not necessary to say much or have answers to questions—just be there to listen and let the family member know you care.

A telephone call a few weeks after the funeral will also prove helpful to the family. This is the time everyone else's life goes back to normal and they stop calling and visiting. The family finds itself alone and feeling deserted. This is a good time to recommend any community support systems that you know are available.

Responsibilities

- Contact family
- Offer help
- Obtain needed information
- Inform family of school procedures
- Help to gather personal items of deceased student
- Attend funeral, if desired
- Keep in contact with family after the funeral
- Recommend available community support systems

☐ The Role of the Media Liaison

The Media Liaison is the person who can present to the public a positive or negative image with regard to the school's response to a death. If the death is one of a sensational nature—such as a shooting, accident, multiple death, or a death recognized prominently in the community—reporters from print, television, and radio are sure to contact the school for information, or to arrive, unannounced, with cameras filming. As unfortunate as it is, the way the media presents a school's handling of a situation may be the only image the public receives.

Experiences have been mixed in schools that have had tragedies which precipitated contact with the press. Some schools felt that the press assisted them and became part of a support effort to help the community. Other schools have had disastrous experiences that developed into an almost adversarial relationship. Again, planning in advance is the key to successful media relations.

Part of the planning process involves whether or not to allow the media in the school or on the school property following an event. As much as many administrators would like to keep members of the media away so as not to have to deal with them, the best advice is to allow them limited access. Designate a location where the reporters, camera, and sound people can gather, set up their equipment, and be addressed as a group by a school representative. Under no circumstances should the press be given free access to the entire school. In one school, a reporter and cameraman entered a counseling room and started filming students talking with counselors. Remember that a school is like a second home, and grieving students and staff members have a right to expect privacy in their grief.

It is a good idea for the Media Liaison to make contact with the various media representatives before a crisis. Having a previous contact and some familiarity with reporters and editors can make contact easier and procedures smoother during a crisis. It is also advantageous to have information regarding the school compiled in a fact sheet prepared and ready to be distributed to the press at your first meeting during an emergency.

Responsibilities

- Make contact with media before crisis
- Contact media when a crisis occurs
- Have media gathering room available
- Keep media from roaming through school
- Prepare school fact sheet before crisis
- Prepare news release in conjunction with principal
- Be the only person to talk to media
- Explain rules for the press clearly, both verbally and in writing
- Explain how media is valuable at the time of tragedy
- Ask for cooperative work environment between media and school
- Be honest with the press

- Be as helpful as possible
- Respect media as professionals
- Understand that you cannot tell reporters how to write or report a story
- Always talk as if everything you say is on the record

☐ The Role of the Teacher

Generally, teachers are the primary school professionals with whom the students develop a relationship. They look to their teachers for information, as role models on how to act, and as valuable support people. This is especially true following a death. How the teacher responds can set the tone for how the student will react and eventually cope with the loss.

The teacher must give his students the most up-to-date information available from his administration. It should be the same information every other teacher gives to the students to avoid confusion and anxiety. Do not speculate with students about unsubstantiated rumors such as the possibility of suicide or the involvement of drugs or alcohol.

It will be necessary for the teacher to modify his lesson plans for a few days. His plans for class should include the opportunity for students to express their feelings, discuss the issues, clarify any misinformation, and instill a feeling of sincerity and caring. The teacher should feel free to express his own feelings to the students.

Teachers must be willing to refer students who seem at risk to the counselors designated by the Crisis Response Team. A student may only need a short period of individual attention to clarify his feelings, or he may need more in-depth therapy to address more serious issues. If additional attention or therapy is needed, the Crisis Response Team counselor will refer the student to the proper professional.

Responsibilities

- Read announcement
- Modify classes
- Talk with students
- Clarify misinformation
- Implement activities to encourage expression of feelings
- Express own feelings
- Give grief information
- Remain nonjudgmental of grief reactions
- Provide activities to encourage remembering deceased
- Make referrals when necessary
- Support students

- Use support resources for self
- Write condolence note to family
- Have in-school and outside resources talk with classes
- Attend funeral, if desired

☐ The Role of the Guidance Counselor

School counselors are often able to talk with and possibly even develop a relationship with some students. The feelings of trust that have developed over time will make it easier for students to express their feelings. The counselor's professional experience will allow him to assess students who have been seen or those who have been referred for help. If, in the counselor's professional opinion, a student is definitely at risk, a referral should be made to the school psychologist or social worker, and the student's family should be notified.

Responsibilities

- Staff Crisis Center
- Talk with students
- Clarify misinformation
- Encourage students to express feelings
- Express own feelings
- Give grief information
- Remain nonjudgmental of grief reaction
- Give priority to referrals
- Support students
- Use support resources for self
- Make referrals to psychologist or physician
- Contact parents if necessary
- Attend funeral, if desired

☐ The Role of the School Psychologist and/or Social Worker

The psychologist or social worker is often the primary in-school referral person. The educational and experiential background of this individual renders him most qualified to carry out or assist outside consultants with in-school counseling of students and staff, providing information and assistance to school staff, completing assessment intervention forms when necessary, and making referrals to the school physician for an at-risk student. If a student's parents have not been notified about their child's vulnerability, the psychologist or social worker should contact them.

Responsibilities

- Make primary referral
- Provide in-school treatment of students
- Provide staff counseling and education
- Complete student assessments
- Make referrals to physician or community agency
- Contact parents
- Attend funeral, if desired

☐ The Role of the School Nurse

By taking care of the students' physical and emotional needs throughout the year, the school nurse will generally develop a good rapport with them. The nursing office or infirmary is neutral territory. It is usually a home-like setting, with a refrigerator, beds, and couch, and students usually feel comfortable and non-threatened there.

The nurse can expect more students to be visiting her after a death has occurred. Many of the students will describe some of the symptoms and grief responses mentioned earlier. Others may just want to talk or lie down. They will be hurting and will not know that grief is causing the pain. The nurse should encourage them to talk and express their feelings, tell them it is okay to feel that way or even to cry, and comfort the pain in their hearts as well as that in their bodies.

If it is determined that a student is at risk, he should be referred to the Crisis Center or school psychologist.

Responsibilities

- Care for physical needs
- Allow students to express emotions
- Provide comfortable location
- Make assessment of students
- Make referrals
- Attend funeral, if desired

☐ The Role of the Librarian

Librarians are often overlooked as an important resource during a crisis such as a death of a student or staff member. However, the library staff is in a position to offer supportive information to the school community. Putting appropriate reading and audiovisual material on reserve for individual or class use can be helpful. Some students will initially seek the privacy of the library, rather than a designated crisis counseling room. An observant librarian can refer or even accompany a student to someone for support.

Responsibilities

- Put appropriate reading and A/V material on reserve
- Listen to students if approached
- Take students to Crisis Center
- Make referrals
- Attend funeral, if desired

☐ The Role of Transportation Personnel

If school bus drivers are notified in a timely manner, they can prevent a possibly upsetting situation from occurring. In one school, the bus driver was not notified that a student had died, and she stopped at the student's house as usual. The parents were upset and called the principal. Also, bus drivers can develop close relationships with students. The caring driver can offer sympathy to a student who is a friend or family member of the deceased. This can mean a lot to a student.

☐ The Role of Support Staff

It is not unusual for support staff members in a school to develop a good relationship with some students. They may be the people with whom a student feels most comfortable talking. If approached, the staff member should listen to what the student has to say and encourage a visit to the Crisis Center. It would be a good idea for the staff member to walk the student to one of the crisis rooms and introduce him or her to the staff person in charge of that room. If the student does not wish to be accompanied to the center, the student's name should be given to a member of the Crisis Response Team.

Responsibilities

- Listen to students if approached
- Take students to Crisis Center
- Make referrals
- Attend funeral, if desired

☐ The Role of the School Physician

By the time a student has been referred to the school physician through the nurse or psychologist, he is usually in need of immediate help. After assessing his physical needs and prescribing treatment, the physician may need to refer the student to a mental health professional or agency. If his parents have not yet been notified as to the condition of the student, the physician should notify them at this time.

Responsibilities

- See students
- Make assessments
- Make referrals
- Contact parents
- Attend funeral service, if desired

☐ Community Resource People

Many schools have found it helpful to have a working relationship with outside professionals who can provide assistance during a crisis period. As stated earlier, these consultants can be paid or they can volunteer. Four groups that have provided support to school staff are grief specialists, mental health professionals, clergy, and funeral directors.

Grief Specialist

This professional can provide invaluable assistance during a death situation. Even if a school has personnel who have some grief-related training, they are usually not specialists or experts in this field. This professional should act in an advisory capacity to the Crisis Response Team. He should also attend staff meetings as either the spokesperson to explain grief-related issues to staff or as an additional resource for the staff members who inform the faculty.

The grief specialist can also talk to classes if requested. If needed, he can provide direct counseling to students or staff. There have been instances where the grief specialist has provided emotional support and counseling to the school counseling staff because they were too emotionally involved to remain objective.

Responsibilities

- Advise Crisis Response Team
- Attend staff meetings
- Provide informational resources for classes, if requested
- Provide counseling to students and/or staff, if necessary

Mental Health Professionals

Mental health professionals should be available to provide counseling or support to staff members in the same manner as the grief specialist. Usually they supplement the school counselors, social workers, and psychologist in staffing crisis centers to provide individual and group support and counseling to students. One of these professionals can also provide long-term follow-up care, if needed.

Responsibilities

- Man counseling rooms
- Provide immediate crisis counseling
- Provide long-term follow-up care, if needed
- Provide assistance to staff, if needed

Clergy

Most clergy are sensitive to people in crisis. They can be a helpful addition to a crisis team during a tragedy. Their role is to offer support and counseling to students and staff if they are trained in this area as would a grief specialist or counselor. Some clergy will readily admit they do not have the expertise for grief counseling and will not accept an invitation to join a team.

Responsibilities

- Staff the crisis room
- Provide counseling support

Funeral Director

A funeral director is in a unique position as a resource to staff and students. He can explain the procedures that will occur during the wake and funeral, and describe appropriate behavior and etiquette during these rituals to students. The funeral director can also prepare people ahead of time for certain aspects that can be upsetting, such as the physical condition of the body of the deceased, and the types of physical outpouring of emotions to expect. He can also organize the logistics of having a large group of students attending the funeral or wake.

Some funeral directors have an educational background in counseling, qualifying them as grief counselors. In this instance, they may be used in the Crisis Center to give support.

Responsibilities

• Explain funeral procedures to staff
• Explain proper funeral behavior to students
• Organize large group attendance at funeral or wake
• Provide grief counseling, if qualified

Responsibility Checklist

Action	Yes	No	Whom
Death information confirmed			
Crisis Team contacted			
Crisis Team meeting scheduled			
Statement to be read by teachers written			
Statement for press written			
Telephone inquiry statement written			
Superintendent notified			
Other school principals notified			
Flag lowered			
Outside consultants contacted			
Staff notified via telephone tree			
Staff meeting scheduled			
Headquarters Room designated			
Crisis Room designated			
Media Room designated			
At-risk students/staff identified			
At-risk students/staff contacted			
Statement read to classes by teachers			
Supportive statement made by principal by intercom			
Staff assigned to crisis rooms			
Grief literature made available in library			
Parents notified of death and school's response			
Deceased's family contacted			
Substitute teachers contacted			
"Tips for Teachers" handout distributed			
"Suggestions for Students" handout distributed			
Additional security contacted			
Letter of condolence to deceased's family sent			
Flowers sent to funeral home			
Funeral director contacted about student visitation			
Students informed about funeral etiquette			
Second staff meeting scheduled			
Student attendance at funeral organized			
Faculty freed up to attend funeral			
School remembrance service planned			
School remembrance service held			
Deceased's belongings collected			
Deceased's belongings given to family			
Evaluation meeting scheduled			
Evaluation report written			

Time Table for Daily Activities

Once the principal has verified the information regarding a death, a meeting of the Crisis Response Team is called. The principal addresses the team and gives them all available information. The team then plans the appropriate level of response that can include the following:

- Notification of staff via phone tree if not during school hours
- Designation of Crisis Center Headquarters and rooms
- Writing of press release (Media Liaison to assist principal)
- Writing of statement to be used as announcement in classes
- Determination of the need for appropriate outside consultants
- Determination of the need for counselors from other schools
- Preparation of hand-out material or gathering of previously prepared material for distribution
- Organization of first staff meeting
- Determination of appropriateness of memorial service

☐ First Emergency Staff Meeting

The faculty and staff will gather at the first emergency staff meeting to be given information regarding the death and the steps the school plans to implement in order to assist the student body. It is also at this meeting that information about grief response will be reviewed and the identification of at-risk students will begin. This is an important meeting, and all available staff should attend. This includes administrative, faculty, support, transportation, maintenance, and security personnel.

The principal should begin the meeting. It is during this gathering that the principal will set the tone for the school's response. Staff will take their lead from the principal. Representatives from the Crisis Response Team should be on the agenda to discuss their role and the crisis response actions to be taken. An experienced and knowledgeable crisis team member, mental health professional, or grief specialist should also be present to discuss grief-related information. Important information should be distributed in writing to everyone. One of the consequences of a crisis situation is that people tend to have a difficult time remembering facts, and the written handouts will be helpful following the meeting.

Principal's Responsibilities

- Give all available facts regarding the death
- Dispel any rumors that may be circulating
- Do not speculate on any aspects of the death for which you are uncertain.
- Relate information on funeral arrangements, if they have been made
- Explain procedural details not being discussed by Crisis Response Team
- Ensure that no one except the Media Liaison gives statements to press
- Determine what announcement to make in classrooms
- Determine whether any substitute teachers are available

Crisis Response Team Representative's Responsibilities

Explain crisis response actions with regard to:

- Crisis rooms and who will be staffing them
- Availability of crisis members to go to classrooms
- Grief-related literature in school library
- Identifying at-risk students

Whenever there is a death on campus, there are certain students who may be expected to take the death harder than others and may require individual attention. It is important to identify these students as soon as possible. Potential categories of at-risk students are:

- Siblings
- Closest friends
- Club or team members of the deceased
- Students who have had difficulty coping with crisis in the past
- Those who have recently experienced any death

- Suicide-prone students
- Classmates from last year

Teacher's Responsibilities

A written outline should be distributed to teachers suggesting possible classroom activities for the next couple of days. A discussion of these suggestions is also appropriate. A list of activities follows. (See Chapter 7 for additional information.)

- Modify lesson plans
- Give facts
- Give location of crisis rooms
- Describe schedule for the day
- Reassure students that help is available
- Encourage verbal expression
- Answer questions
- Write about deceased's death
- Do drawings
- Write condolence letters
- Stress that it's okay to cry, and that hugs are okay, too
- Talk individually when needed
- Refer at-risk students
- Refer students who request help
- Have no expectations
- Be non-judgmental
- Plan funeral attendance

Grief Specialist's Responsibilities

- Address grief responses of students
- Address grief responses of staff
- Make suggestions for responding to grieving students
- Encourage staff to discuss their own feelings
- Be available to talk to staff individually

☐ After First Staff Meeting

Principal's Responsibilities

- Write press release and send to media.
- After teachers have had time to inform classes about the death and

available help, a general statement over the public address system can be given. This should include relaying feelings of sympathy, the school's commitment to help, and general encouragement.

- Assist or direct as necessary the organization and staffing of crisis headquarters.
- Write and send condolence letter to family.
- Contact student leaders and inform them of school's response.

Crisis Response Team's Responsibilities

- Organize crisis rooms
- Assist with organization of crisis headquarters
- Meet with counseling staff to discuss staffing of crisis rooms
- Notify librarian to make available appropriate literature
- Meet with students or staff requesting individual help
- Talk individually with at-risk students and refer when necessary
- Reserve Media Room
- Contact family of deceased (Family Liaison)

☐ End-of-Day Meeting

- Principal gives staff any new facts
- Crisis Response Team updates staff on use of crisis rooms
- General information given, if available
- Staff shares experiences
- Additional at-risk students identified
- Staff allowed and encouraged to express feelings
- Helpful suggestions given by Crisis Response Team or consultants
- Next day activities discussed

☐ Day Two

- Additional information given to staff in written form by principal
- Additional information given to staff in written form by Crisis Response Team
- Crisis rooms are staffed
- Media is notified of steps being taken by school
- Family of deceased contacted and given an update on school activities
- Students are seen by nurse, guidance counselors, school psychologist, or social workers as requested or referred

- At-risk students are identified and referred
- Classes are still flexible with more classroom work included

☐ After-Class Staff Meeting

- Staff allowed and encouraged to express feelings
- Staff shares experiences
- New at-risk students identified
- Report on at-risk students (generalized, maintaining confidentiality)
- Information given on funeral plan
- Funeral director may address group to inform about funeral
- Any family requests given

☐ Day Three

If the funeral is on this day, the staff and students who have been given approval may attend the funeral. After the funeral, those who attended can meet at the school to share feelings and defuse or debrief. After this, do not expect full attention or participation by staff or students when they return to class.

For those who did not attend the funeral, classes are held. Feelings can be discussed as needed and class work is included.

If the funeral is not held on this day, follow the schedule for Day Two. The number of counselors in the Crisis Room can begin to decrease. More class work can be included in classrooms.

Helping Grieving Students

The school is a center for sharing ideas, testing new concepts, and learning new phenomena. Thus, it should be a safe place to confront and deal with death-related issues and provide appropriate learning and curricular experiences.

☐ Before a Death

In recent years, some schools have implemented formal approaches to death education for children as curricular components. Other schools address the topic of death as needed in response to a significant crisis or as a "teachable moment" occurrence following a death that impacts a child or several children.

There are numerous initiatives teachers can launch toward addressing the concepts of dying and death within the school setting. A few of these curricular experiences are identified here. If addressed properly, they can be extremely useful in assisting a child or numbers of children confronted with death as well as promoting a better understanding of death as an essential element of the life cycle (Case & Case, 1995). Teachers should:

- Develop short pedagogical units that focus on death, and encourage healthy class discussions and student interaction.
- Utilize newspaper stories for the purpose of discussing the life cycle of plants, animals, and human beings. Many aspects of dying and death can be addressed appropriately in health education units.

- Make brief library assignments on relevant topics and have students do written assignments and oral reports.
- Select appropriate books for students that deal effectively with loss, read selections to them, and have them read selected topics.
- Participate in selected field trips, i.e., funeral homes and cemeteries, provided they are appropriately planned and approved by school administrators and parents.
- Invite experts within the community to speak on relevant topics. Such excellent resources include funeral directors, doctors, nurses, other health care providers, ministers, lawyers, and professors.

☐ How Teachers Can Help

Teachers are uniquely positioned to guide grieving students and their classmates. But, like many people in our society, teachers often feel uncomfortable discussing death and loss. This reluctance can adversely affect the children in their charge who look to their teachers for truth, knowledge, and support (Naierman, 1997). Holland and Ludford (1995) indicate that their research in primary schools showed that while teachers attempt to support bereft students, few have any formal bereavement training. To compensate for this, teachers should take every opportunity available to learn about the grieving process in adults and children.

When many students in a school are affected by a crisis, the classroom may be the primary setting in which they begin to cope with personal reactions. It can provide the continuity and security of a safe place that a grieving student may desperately need. A firm hand that establishes boundaries may be a comforting one, and consistency can be a sign of normalcy in a student's off-balance life (Naierman, 1997).

The extent to which students convey their feelings depends upon the climate of the classroom. Trust and rapport can be established as teachers discuss illness and death among other topics on a regular basis. Providing children with accurate information helps prevent misconceptions and disturbing associations that can complicate reactions to death and loss (Schonfeld, 1993).

There is an agreement among authors that much can be done to help students adjust to the death of a member of the school community. The following suggestions are adapted from Glass (1990), Klicker (1993), Pitcher and Poland (1992), Postel (1986), and are appropriate in any grief-related situation in or outside of school.

- The death must be acknowledged. Give the students the facts as they are known. Share accurate information, including the cause, time and place of death, as well as funeral plans.

- Rumors can run rampant following an unexpected death. Do not speculate about facts that are not known to be true. Give honest answers to questions.
- Encourage students to express their feelings.
- Let students know that it is normal to grieve and to have different types of feelings, ranging from intense pain to not being affected at all. Explain common grief responses they may experience.
- Give them permission to grieve, or not to grieve: some students may feel uncomfortable because they are not responding like the others.
- Any questions the students have should be answered truthfully.
- Use the words "death," "dying," and "dead," not euphemisms such as "passed away."
- When talking with students, refer to the deceased by name, try to remember him accurately, and do not idealize him.
- It's okay for staff to share their own feelings with students. It's also okay to cry in front of them. Be honest. If you are angry, afraid, or guilty, let them know why. Staff can be role models for appropriate grieving.
- Reassure the students that anger, guilt, sadness, and tears are normal responses to loss. Let them know that a person can be very sad even though he may not be crying.
- Help the students to determine whether any guilt they are experiencing is justified. Remind them that they are only human and that we all continue to learn as we experience life.
- Explain to the students that they may experience high and low feelings, and that using alcohol or drugs will only delay the grieving process.
- Don't be judgmental. Don't judge a student's response or compare it to others' responses. Respect the validity of all feelings expressed.
- Reassure the students. Let the students know about all the help that is available for them within the school.
- Don't use a phrase like "I know how you feel." You don't know how they feel. You only know how you feel. Studies have shown that this particular phrase often upsets the bereaved.
- Don't put a time frame on their grieving. It takes as long or as short a time as it takes.
- Be aware of the students' intellectual and emotional limitations for understanding death.
- Suggest various readings related to death, loss, and grief. Ask younger children if they would like such a story read to them.
- Provide an opportunity for students who want to talk openly to do so. For those who find it difficult to verbalize feelings, let them draw or write about what they are feeling or something about the deceased.

- Teachers can keep classes flexible for a few days following a crisis. Use this time together to discuss such topics as the event, death in general, student experiences with other deaths, and their fears or anxieties.
- Writing a symbolic note to the deceased can promote a sense of closure for some students. Sympathy notes to the family of the deceased can be a comfort to the author and recipient as well. If notes are to be given to the family, they should be reviewed to ensure that no rude or crude remarks are included.
- Older students may want to plan a more concrete activity such as participation in the funeral or memorial service. They can take up a collection for a memorial donation to a charity or for flowers. Some schools have dedicated the yearbook to the deceased or planted a tree in his name.
- Let the students decide what should happen to the deceased student's desk. One middle school teacher discovered that by leaving the desk in the classroom, it became a link to the deceased, which helped the class members reflect on the events and recover from the loss.
- Teachers can offer structure, care, and support to students who may not receive it at home or anywhere else.

☐ What Teachers Have Found to Be Successful

It can be tremendously helpful to hear about the techniques of teachers who have worked with children when a death occurred in the school community. Katherine Curro, a 5th grade teacher at McKenney Middle School in Canton, New York, offers the following summary of approaches and activities that have worked for teachers in a wide variety of settings. You are encouraged to let these suggestions stimulate your own ideas and lead you to adaptations that will work for the age and nature of your students.

The chance to discuss questions with someone who is patient and rational can provide an important emotional base for a healthy concept of death. A teacher who cannot handle the discussion needs to find a school nurse, counselor, or funeral director who can, and to make sure that this person will be available on an as-needed basis.

Beginning the Discussion of Death

Following are several discussion-starters with which to broach the topic of death:

"Boys and girls, Bobby is sad this morning because his puppy was killed by a car last night. Some of you know how hurt Bobby is feeling because you have lost pets, too. What can we say to Bobby today to let him know we care?"

"Class, I've asked you to meet in our circle this morning because I have to tell you some bad news: Joanne is not at school today because her father died. Some of you know how scared Joanne has been about his illness. Even though doctors did their best to help him, he was too sick to get well. Let's talk for a minute about the way this makes us feel."

"Children, this won't be a usual day for any of us. I don't think this is a day we'll feel much like doing math and reading. Whenever I look at Darren's empty seat, I think of what he would be doing and saying if he were still alive. I'd like to tell him that I liked him a lot, that he had good ideas, and a great sense of humor. Most of all, I want him to know that when I was strict with him, I still liked him. Do you have anything you wish you could tell Darren?"

Relieving Guilt

Very young children believe in the magical properties of language and may be convinced that their words have the power to cause harm to people. Guilt is common following a death, as children recall pushing a classmate or taking his toy. Older children, too, may suffer from memories of making rude remarks, taunting, or terrorizing their classmate. Also, guilt may arise from having ignored or rejected a sick classmate.

Some teachers have found success in having classroom ceremonies where children think of things that they would like to say to the student who has died. The student's chair can be arranged as the focus for this. A variation that works for older children is having them write letters to their classmate.

Reassurance

It's a developmental fact that most young children are self-centered. A typical reaction to death for six- and seven-year-old students is anxiety. They ask or think, "Will this happen to me?" Obvious opportunities for safety lessons are present if a child has died from some kind of preventable accident. Reassurance about the nature and rarity of most childhood diseases can help in other instances. However, it is important not to blanket students with assurances such as "This can't happen to you." Acknowledging death as something that is a part of life confirms the truth that children are just beginning to perceive for themselves.

Some teachers have found that bereavement is a time when children take extra solace in eating familiar foods. In several classrooms where a death has occurred, cooking projects have brought a feeling of togetherness, eased tensions, and encouraged conversation. Simple recipes work best.

When Talking is Not Enough

Students may go through a period of suppressed activity, maybe even speaking in whispers, which is usually followed by a release of emotional tension, often manifesting itself in rather wild behavior. The time frame for such a reaction depends on the age and nature of the group. In contrast to other stages in the grieving process, this is a time when talk will be difficult (too much adrenaline is in the way).

Being out of doors calms children. Large motor activities like swimming, running, skating, or hiking work well. Organized sports generally require greater focus and cooperation than children can muster at this point.

Physical Closeness

Physical closeness such as hugging, touching, and handholding are very important to most bereaved children. Older children may wish to change their seating arrangement into a circle or devise some other way to reduce the feelings of loneliness that death brings.

Celebrating the Person Who Was

Some classes, whether elementary, middle, or high school, are more ready for and interested in ceremonies and memorials than others. In cases where the deceased student was very ill, absent from school for prolonged periods, or difficult to get along with, such activities may be inappropriate. A memorial that is forced is of little value. However, if the student who died was greatly liked and sadly missed, spontaneous affirmations of the person can have a galvanizing effect on the entire group.

Some elementary school classes have enjoyed putting together a scrapbook about their friend. Older students may want to write personal notes or poems. Some have published these writings or sent them to the student's family.

One class found a constructive outlet for their grief for a classmate who had died of cystic fibrosis. These sixth graders organized a school-wide bike-a-thon to raise money for research and treatment of the disease. The class plans to make this an annual event until it graduates.

When Only One Child is Grieving

It's particularly hard for teachers to choose a course of action when the bereavement involves only one child. Most teachers report that bereaved children feel a need to be with the group. Separating them, even for the purpose of excusing them from work responsibilities, generally causes anxiety. A student's need to feel the support of classmates does not have to mean that lessons stop for everyone during the entire day. Some ideas to try include:

For younger students:

- A group hug.
- A chance to be the teacher's helper for the day.
- A buddy system.
- A pass to visit someone at school when the student feels the need to talk. It could be the counselor, the principal, or even a custodian or cafeteria worker. It is especially apt to be last year's teacher if the death occurs early in the fall.
- The chance to express feelings by drawing or working with art materials.
- A one-to-one or group read-aloud, perhaps using a title from the bibliography.

For older students:

- An understanding talk between teacher and student.
- A comforting handshake or hand on the shoulder.
- Allowing privacy at times when the student feels emotional and embarrassed.
- Condolence notes from classmates.
- Attendance at the funeral by teachers and classmates.
- Flexibility with arrangements and tasks.

☐ Defusing

In instances when students have been a part of an event that has been life-threatening, injury-producing, or emotionally traumatizing, participating in a defusing process can usually help. The following information has been adapted from *How to Help Children After a Disaster, A Guidebook for Teachers* (1991). This guidebook was developed by the Alameda County (California) Mental Health Services under a grant from the Federal Emergency Management Administration.

Defusing is a supportive, personalized, safe, *interactive* process between individuals in small groups with facilitator(s) that provides and facilitates clarity and complete expression of the event and its accompanying experiences. It can be emotional, but it can also help children to develop coping skills and heal.

The defusing process is most effective when it is carried out in the following sequence:

1. Discussion of general disastrous events. Children are asked to talk about violence in schools in general.
2. Discussion of specific disastrous event experiences. Children are encouraged to talk about the event that took place at the school.
3. Discussion of personal experiences. Students talk about their personal experience with the shooting.

The following questions can be used to facilitate dialogue:

- Where were you when it (disaster/event) happened?
- What were you doing?
- Where were your friends?
- Where was your family (if disaster was something like a hurricane)?
- What was your first thought when it happened?
- What were you thinking during it?

Teachers should allow for silence for students with poor language skills, shyness, discomfort, etc. Peer support for these children should be encouraged. If a child has low English skills, consider asking for a translator or a peer to help the child express his feelings in words. Create the opportunity for verbal expression in any language.

- What did you see?
- What did you hear?
- What sound did it make? (Allow for yelling, etc. to allow the students to make sounds.)
- What did you smell?
- What did you do after it?
- How did you respond?
- How did you feel?
- What did other people around you do (during, after)?
- What was the silliest thing you did?

- What dreams did you have after it? (Note: dreams could be related or unrelated; either is fine to discuss.)
- What reminds you of it? When do you think about it?
- What do you do differently since the (disaster/event)?
- How do you feel now (re: the disaster memories)?
- What makes you feel better?
- Was anyone you know killed in the event?
- How have you gotten through rough times before?
- What would you do differently if it happened again?
- How did you help others? How would you help next time?

Remember, the goal of this process is to help children to feel better. These are not the only questions that can be asked. You may think of similar questions that are appropriate for the event with which you are confronted. The questions should be open-ended so they cannot be answered with only a yes or no. Open-ended questions are preferred because they facilitate verbal expression.

Most of the above questions would be helpful at any time following a disastrous event from one day after to one or more years following it. Remember to keep yourself in a facilitative, guiding role, not in a role of controlling the discussion.

☐ Ongoing Support

It is not unusual for schools, even those that respond well after a death, to be more reactive than proactive. Most schools wait until a crisis strikes to react with assistance. An improvement on this system would be to incorporate continuous death-related activities throughout the year, both in and out of the classroom.

Wolfelt (1995) offers excellent advice to teachers for incorporating death-related material into their lesson plans. He counsels teachers to keep in mind that grief is a process, not an event. In the weeks and months to come after the death, you will need to provide ongoing opportunities for your students to express their grief. Do not wait until a student's parents are killed in a car accident to teach your class about death and grief. Make lesson plans that incorporate these important topics into the curriculum. And use natural, everyday encounters with death—a run-over squirrel, a car accident that made local headlines—to talk about your students' fears and concerns.

All adults should remember the concepts of the "teachable moment" and "created moment." The teachable moment occurs when an opportunity to teach children about life and death arises through events happening around them: a baby is born, a classmate's grandfather dies. When these events occur, make positive use of them by talking openly about them. The created moment means working to create regular opportunities to teach children about death rather than waiting for "one big tell all" concerning death to occur.

Children who have already been acquainted with the naturalness and permanence of death are more likely to grieve in healthy ways when someone they love dies.

Outside the classroom, the school can provide a continuous source of support by forming a support group for grieving students. Elder (1994) believes that support groups can help students in the following ways:

- Demonstrate to young people that they are not alone in their grief.
- Provide information about, and a framework for, making sense of both death-related experiences and experiences of grief and mourning.
- Help identify, validate, and normalize strong feelings and other unusual experiences which are associated with loss, grief, and mourning.
- Provide permission and a safe place in which to confront and express those feelings.
- Emphasize the positive legacy that endures from a lost relationship.
- Suggest constructive ways in which to remember and memorialize a life that is now dead.
- Demonstrate in non-judgmental ways the conviction or trust that life and living can and do go on, by producing mentors and temporary role models and acting out options or different ways in which individuals can find "new normals" in their lives.

The third component of an ongoing support system is for the school staff to be aware that:

- Grief can be long-lasting, in some cases for two years or more.
- Grief can be cumulative. Individuals experiencing multiple losses can suffer grief overload, which can affect their normal behavior and functioning. Losses are not always caused by death. They can be caused by divorce, separation, relocation, when friends or loved ones move away, or by loss of a family's home due to accident or natural disaster.
- Grief that seems to be under control can resurface around special days, such as birthdays, holidays, or the anniversary of a death.

☐ When a Student Has a Life-Threatening Illness

A Wish with Wings, Inc. of Arlingtion, Texas conducted a survey of 61 parents of children who had cancer or other chronic illnesses. Among the questions posed were "How can teachers be most helpful when a sick child reenters school?" and "What have teachers done that is least helpful?" Highlights of answers appear below.

The Best Teachers (A Parent's View) . . .

1. Call or visit my child during times of absence.
2. Know that parents need a little TLC, too. Cards, phone calls, visits—all are appreciated.
3. Listen to my concerns and fears.
4. Take time to become familiar with treatments given to my child and their effect on school performance.
5. Visit with my child before re-entry to talk about any fears she/he may have.
6. Adjust regular lesson plans to account for change in child's ability to complete lengthy tasks or assignments.
7. Gently encourage my child to reach his/her *current* potential.
8. Follow my doctor's and my instructions regarding bathroom visits, snacks, wearing a hat, etc.
9. Accept the sometimes hard-to-accept side effects of cancer or its treatments (slurring words, falling asleep in class, diminished temper control, ability to accept discipline, etc.).
10. Are supportive of us during setbacks of the illness.
11. Encourage classmates to call or write my child during periods of extended absence.
12. Prepare the class for physical and emotional changes in my child as a consequence of treatment; suggest ways to be helpful.
13. Treat my child as normally as possible, given the restrictions imposed by disease and its treatment; don't impose their own limits.
14. Are supportive and encouraging, but not phony in their praise.
15. Know when a situation is over their heads and call the parents, doctor, or administrators for help.
16. Include my child in as many class functions as possible. She/he may not have the stamina for a full day of school, but may be able to come to the holiday party or class outing.

The Worst Teachers (A Parent's View) . . .

1. Show fear about having my child in their class.
2. Allow pity for him or her within the classroom.
3. Fail to share information about my child's appearance, special needs, etc., with colleagues, substitutes, and aides.

4. Convey an attitude that assumes my child won't be able to do things.
5. Fail to educate themselves about the disease, its treatments, and possible changes in a child's appearance, mannerisms, etc.
6. Make an issue of my child's differences in front of the whole class.
7. Ignore problems classmates have in adjusting to their friend's disease, which may manifest as teasing, mimicking, etc.
8. Fail to give my child an opportunity to at least try whatever the others are doing.
9. Fail to give my child the benefit of the doubt whenever possible on assignments and homework.

Parents' Comments

"Do whatever you have to do inside yourself to become genuinely welcoming and comfortable that first day back. This will set the tone for the entire class."

"Explain the child's disease and what she/he is going through, but don't be a downer and dwell on the possibility of death."

"My son had no hair for five months. One day at recess, an older student came up and knocked off his hat. He was humiliated by the laughter. But his classmates, who had been prepared by the teacher, stood up for him."

"My son wanted to wear a hooded sweatshirt on his first day back at school because he had lost is hair. When he arrived, five other students were wearing on hooded sweatshirts, too. The teacher had enlisted them to make him part of the crowd. IT WORKED!"

"The entire staff was helpful to us. When we went to the airport to leave for Justin's bone marrow transplant, the principal came to see us off and gave us his home telephone number."

"Our kids need *empathy*, not *sympathy*."

Used by permission. A Wish with Wings, Inc., Arlington, TX.

CHAPTER

Teaching Students How to Behave in Grief-Related Situations

The following information was prepared by Ken Roach, a school psychologist for the Chesterfield County Public Schools (State). It is found in *Resource Guide for Crisis Management in Schools* and reproduced here with the permission of the Virginia Department of Education, Office of Compensatory Programs. Each section is designed to be used as a handout for students.

☐ Helping a Grieving Friend

First Steps

- If you learn that a friend is grieving outside of school hours, call and go to his home as quickly as you can, if possible, or at least call.
- If you learn of a grieving friend during school, try to see the friend or send a note until you are able to talk.
- Your presence is all that is needed; if you wish to take a flower or anything else that might be meaningful, that's all right, too.
- Offer physical comfort.
- Don't be afraid to cry with your friend.
- Do not try to take the pain away from your grieving friend.

Communication

- Talk about the deceased person. (Grieving people really like telling stories about the deceased, beginning with story starters such as "Do you remember the time . . . ".)
- Don't use cliché statements. (e.g., "He's better off now since he now has no pain.")
- Don't be afraid you will upset your friend more by asking or talking about the deceased.
- Just sitting with your friend may be all that's needed at times. Don't be afraid of silence—the griever will most likely fill it with talking about the deceased.
- Offer suggestions only when advice is asked.
- Listen, no matter what the topic.
- Do not tell the griever to feel better since there are other loved ones still alive.
- Call periodically to check on the person.

Attending a Visitation or Funeral at the Funeral Home

- If you have never been to a funeral home or funeral, expect to feel nervous.
- Go with a friend or ask a parent to accompany you if this would make you feel more comfortable.
- If this is the first time you've seen the grieving friend, simply offer your condolences. Just saying, "I am sorry about _____'s death" will probably begin a conversation, or simply point out something that was special to you regarding the deceased.
- If the visitation or funeral has an open casket, view the physical remains if you want to; you do not have to.

Later Involvement

- Ask your grieving friend to go places with you, and do activities together. (It's all right if he initially resists.)
- If invitations are turned down, keep inviting.
- Call to check on and talk to your friend.
- Continue to talk about the deceased from time to time.

Reproduced from Resource Guide for Crisis Management in Schools. *Permission granted by Virginia Department of Education.*

☐ Helping Grieving Parents

This information should be helpful when interacting with the parents of a deceased friend. Always respect the wishes of grieving parents. These suggestions must fit the parents' needs and requests.

First Steps

- In the vast majority of cases, the parents very much want to see the friends of their deceased child. They find it comforting.
- If you were a close friend of the deceased and you know the parents, visit them at their home.
- If you were a friend but had not met the parents (but they know who you are), you might still visit the home.
- Other friends might wait until the visitation, such as one held at a funeral home, or wait until the funeral.
- Regardless of the depth of your relationship with the parents, let them hear from you either by a phone call or note.

Communication

- When you visit, do not worry about what to say; your presence is all that is needed. If you wish to take a flower or anything else that might be meaningful, that's all right, too.
- Don't be afraid that you will upset the parents more by asking or talking about the deceased.
- Don't be afraid to cry with the parents.
- Just sitting with the parents may be all that's needed at times. Don't be afraid of silence—the parents will most likely fill the silence talking about their deceased child.
- Offer physical comfort.
- Listen, no matter what the topic.
- If you were a very close friend, the parents might be pleased for you to visit the deceased friend's room.
- Ask what you can do for them, and ask other relatives what you might do to help.
- Do not try to take the pain away from the grieving parents.
- Don't make cliché statements. (e.g., "He's better off now since he now has no pain.")
- Talk about the deceased person. (Grieving people really like telling stories about the deceased, "Do you remember the time . . . ".)
- Offer suggestions only when advice is solicited.
- Do not tell the parents to feel better since there are other children and loved ones still alive.

Attending a Visitation or Funeral at the Funeral Home

- Expect to feel nervous when going to a funeral home or a funeral.
- Go with a friend or ask a parent to accompany you.
- If this is the first time you've seen the parents, simply offer your condolences; just saying, "I am so sorry about _____'s death" will probably begin a conversation; or it may be better to simply point out something that was special to you regarding the deceased.
- If the visitation or funeral has open casket, view the physical remains if you want to; you do not have to.

Later Involvement

- After the funeral, continue to visit the parents. They will probably continue to want to see the friends of the deceased child.
- Call to check on and talk to the parents.
- Continue to talk about their deceased child from time to time.

Reproduced from Resource Guide for Crisis Management in Schools. *Permission granted by Virginia Department of Education.*

☐ When a Teacher is Grieving

Feelings

- You and your classmates should expect to experience different feelings, ranging from shock, sadness, and vulnerability ("This could happen to me or someone I know") to detached, or nothing at all. All feelings are okay.
- Some in your class may even laugh because they are nervous hearing or talking about grief and death. This may be their way of handling it, so don't become angry.
- Don't be surprised to catch yourself asking how this might affect you, your grades, or your relationship with your teacher.
- It's okay to think about other people who have died.

What to Do

- Talk with somebody (a friend or parent) about what has happened. This helps make the situation more real and keeps you from holding everything in.
- Try to summon the courage to communicate with your teacher.

Communicating with Your Grieving Teacher

- Your teacher probably has a lot to do and cannot take calls from students.
- Buy or make a card and send it.
- Write a note (don't feel that you have to use fancy stationery).
- Expect to feel weird trying to write to somebody who is grieving.
- Just writing "I'm sorry," or "I'm thinking about you," or "I hope you are okay" is enough.
- Others may write more, even share their own experiences with grief. One student even composed a poem!
- There is nothing you can say that could make your grieving teacher feel worse.
- You are not going to remind a grieving person that he has had somebody die.
- Your teacher may never throw your card or note away—that's how important your communication will be. Your parents probably still have notes they've received.

Flowers and Donations

- Sending flowers or donations is appropriate, but not required.
- If you really want to do something, you and some friends could pitch in together, or you could organize the class to do something as a group. It takes only one person to organize this.

If You See Your Teacher in the Community

- If you see your teacher at the grocery store, a part of you will want to hide. But think of how will that make your teacher feel.
- Speak to your teacher! You don't have to say much. "How are you doing?" or "We miss you at school" is enough.

Attending Funerals and Memorial Services

- You have to respect the wishes of grieving people.
- Some teachers may welcome students. Others may not feel ready to cope with them. Some may feel uncomfortable with having you around and their being "out of control." You have to understand and respect their needs.

- Sometimes there is no chance to talk with the family. At other times, you can't leave the building without doing so.
- If given the opportunity, speak. Again, just say "I'm sorry" or something brief. Choose your first several words ahead of time to lessen your fear.

Visitation at a Funeral Home

- If students are invited, go if you'd like, but take someone with you.
- Unless you have experience with visitation, you are going to feel scared or weird.
- If you go, speak simply as described above.

Reproduced from Resource Guide for Crisis Management in Schools. *Permission granted by Virginia Department of Education.*

☐ When a Grieving Teacher Returns

Getting Ready

- Plan some type of simple welcome back signal from the class for your grieving teacher. Consider a card signed by all class members; a small banner from "second period"; or some flowers from a parent's yard or a small, inexpensive bouquet.
- If you have not communicated with your teacher, it's not too late to have a note read just from you. It could be waiting in the teacher's mailbox upon his return to school.
- Realize that the same person who left will return. Your teacher may initially seem a little distant or preoccupied, but this should not last too long.
- Your teacher may have very poor concentration for awhile after returning to work. He might repeat things. You may have to repeat your questions.
- Do not expect tests and homework to be returned as quickly as before: poor concentration, low motivation, and fatigue are typical grief reactions.

On the Big Day

- Expect to feel nervous. Your teacher will feel the same way.
- Your teacher also will probably feel strange.

- A part of you will want to sneak into the classroom without being seen. You might even justify these feelings by not wanting to upset your teacher. How would your teacher feel if no one spoke to him? How would you feel if you had been away from school for awhile and no one spoke to you when you returned?
- When you first see your teacher, say something simple, like "Welcome back."
- The class could also even let a very brave volunteer speak for the class to formally welcome your teacher back, or the volunteer could present a card.
- Show good behavior and use your best listening skills. Help your teacher out; it will be a tough day. Smile!
- Some teachers will return quickly to teaching; others will discuss their grief. There is no single right way.

What if Your Teacher Cries?

- You do not have to do anything but be patient.
- Your class could have a brave volunteer designated to offer comfort by saying something simple, such as "We support you."
- The student closest to the tissue box should take the box to the teacher. This shows the class cares and that it's okay to cry.
- At the end of class, students might individually offer brief words of comfort and encouragement, such as "It's okay to get upset" or "I'm glad you are back."
- Crying may embarrass your teacher, but crying can be very helpful.
- If your teacher is having a really bad day, let your guidance counselor or other faculty member know.

Reproduced from Resource Guide for Crisis Management in Schools. *Permission granted by Virginia Department of Education.*

☐ When a Grieving Classmate Returns

First Words

- The classmate probably will feel like he is from a different planet when returning to school.
- There is very little you can say that's wrong, so talk to the classmate.
- At least say "Hello," "Welcome back," "I'm glad to see you," or something similar.

- The brave might even say: "I missed you. I'm so sorry to hear about your _____'s death."
- Even braver friends might even make statements like "It must be incredibly tough to have your _____ die."
- Another option is to write a brief note.
- If your classmate cries, it's okay. You did not cause the grief, and you can't make the person feel worse. Offer comfort and a tissue.

Helping the Classmate Adjust to Class

- Offer to provide past notes.
- Offer to provide notes for comparison for the next week or so. (Your classmate's attention span will probably vary for several weeks.)
- Give the classmate your phone number to call if having problems with homework.
- Ask your classmate if you can call to check on how homework is going.
- Ask the teacher if you can be the student's helper for a week.
- Offer to study together in person or over the phone; this might help with both motivation (grieving students frequently do not feel like doing schoolwork) and concentration.

Some Don'ts

- Don't shun.
- Don't use cliché statements such as "I know how you feel" when nobody knows the unique relationship the classmate had with the deceased.
- Don't expect the person to snap back into his "old self."
- Don't be surprised if the classmate seems unaffected by the loss; everybody has his own way of grieving.
- Don't be afraid to ask appropriate questions about the deceased, like "What did you and your _____ enjoy together?" People never tire of talking about the people they grieve.
- Just because the classmate may seem to be adjusting to school again, don't assume the grieving has stopped, nor the need for comfort and help.

Reproduced from Resource Guide for Crisis Management in Schools. *Permission granted by Virginia Department of Education.*

CHAPTER

Helping Yourself Through Grief

For most of us, there are very few events in our lives that cause as much emotional pain as the death of someone we care about. For those of us involved in the educational system who have experienced the death of one of our students, we know the heartache it can cause.

As much as we are concerned about how the students in school will be able to cope with the loss, we must also be concerned about ourselves. This concern for oneself is often difficult for educators because our lives are devoted to helping and caring for our students. What many of us fail to realize is that before we can really help our students through such a crisis, we must help ourselves so that we have the emotional and physical strength it takes to help them.

The following suggestions are adapted from the *Hope for the Bereaved Handbook*, a publication from Hope for the Bereaved, a Syracuse, New York grief center, and can help you focus your attention and energy inward so you can better prepare yourself for dealing with the crisis and for being a role model for your students. Your role-modeling behavior can be the first experience your students will have for learning healthy ways to deal with grief caused by death.

☐ Learn About Grief Beforehand

Once you learn the dynamics of grief, you will understand on an intellectual level what to expect and why you and your students are responding in certain ways.

☐ Don't Compare Your Grief with Others

There is no right or wrong way to grieve; each of us grieves in our own way. If you think you are grieving more or less, or longer or shorter than others, you may be right, but it's okay.

☐ Don't Keep a Stiff Upper Lip

Two of the worst comments are "Be strong" and "Don't cry." It's okay to cry. Crying does make you feel better. It is even okay if students see you cry. This pertains to males as well as females. This is not a time for men to show how macho they think they are.

☐ Go Easy on Yourself

Don't get upset with yourself if you can't concentrate, or if you feel angry, anxious, afraid, or depressed. Grief does this to us. You probably won't be as productive as usual and your nerves may be on edge. Don't be surprised if the feelings get carried over into your out-of-school life. However, if you are not as upset as others, don't condemn yourself for not reacting. Remember, grief is an individual response.

☐ Don't Take On a New Responsibility Right Away

Your body and mind need rest during grief. You may find it easier to become overwhelmed by work following a loss.

☐ Don't Give Yourself a Time Limit

One mistake people often make is feeling they should return to normal immediately after the funeral. You may feel some pain for weeks or months after. Something might trigger a recurrence of emotion, even a year later. There is no time schedule to which you must adhere.

☐ Talk About How You Feel

Don't keep your feelings bottled up inside yourself. If you can't talk to your colleagues or family, find a counselor at your local hospice, grief support agency, church, synagogue. Seek out an understanding friend, another bereaved person, or a support group member.

☐ Complete Unfinished Business with the Deceased

One of the tragedies of a sudden, unexpected death is that we don't always have the time to say what we wish we should have said when the person was alive. Put your feelings down on paper in a note or a letter to the deceased. Place it in the casket, if possible, bury it someplace, or burn it. It may be more meaningful if you create a little private ceremony. This may seem weird, but most people who try this report feeling better afterwards.

☐ Tranquilizers and Alcohol Won't Stop the Pain— They Will Only Delay It

Coping with grief is best done when you are straight and sober.

☐ Accept Help

Don't be afraid to ask for help, and accept help and support when it is offered. It's okay to need comforting and to seek out understanding and caring people. Join a support group if you think that may help.

☐ Feel What You Feel

You don't choose your emotions, they choose you. Anger, depression, and physical problems are common to those in grief. Thinking you are going crazy is a very normal grief reaction. You are not losing your mind, you are only reacting to the death. Be good to yourself—get plenty of rest, good nutrition, and moderate exercise. Put balance into your life. Rest, work, and relax.

CHAPTER

The Funeral and School Remembrance Activities

☐ The Funeral

The value for the bereaved of attending the viewing and funeral of the deceased has been documented extensively in the literature (Doka, 1995; Grollman, 1993; Fitzgerald, 1992; Morgan, 1990; Schaefer & Lyons, 1986; Worden, 1996). The funeral is overwhelmingly considered a valuable ritual in helping the bereaved adjust to the loss of a loved one (Klicker, 1997).

For many, seeing the dead body is the only tangible affirmation they have that the person has really died. In such cases, seeing truly is believing. It is a powerful and helpful first step in adjusting to the death of someone they love. Aside from providing this visual confirmation of death, the funeral offers support and comfort in a variety of ways:

As a final disposition for the body of the deceased. One of the harsh realities of death is the necessity for the final disposition of the physical body of the deceased. This final disposition, whether it is burial, cremation, or entombment, can be accomplished with as much or as little ceremony as desired.

As a religious ritual. Religion has a prominent position in many people's lives. They receive comfort and reassurance in religious beliefs and ceremonies. For most people, the funeral is principally a religious ceremony that allows them to fulfill the final phase of their spiritual life.

As a means of social support. The pain of grief is never more intense than when experienced alone. The coming together of friends and family to pay tribute to the deceased and give respects to the survivors provides comfort to all who experience it. Although some people feel awkward or frightened when attending a funeral, almost everyone feels a sense of belonging when expressing condolences, offering acts of concern, and supporting the survivors. This same sense of community and caring is felt by the survivors, along with a sense of pride that others respected the deceased enough to attend the funeral.

As a celebration of life. Everyone, no matter how famous or unknown, rich or poor, young or old, affects the lives of others and contributes to the life of his family and community in some way. The funeral may be the only opportunity for an organized reflection and recognition of this life.

As an acceptable environment for the expression of feelings. Many people, including students, find it difficult to express their feelings in public. They worry about appearances or feel embarrassed. The funeral is a venue in which you are encouraged to openly express your feelings. You are in an atmosphere where everyone is experiencing similar feelings and where the social taboo of crying in public does not apply.

☐ Should Students Attend the Funeral or Wake?

There is a general agreement among mental health experts that going to a funeral can be a positive experience for children. However, they should never be forced to attend. The student's level of involvement at the funeral should also be an individual decision. Some students will participate in all ceremonies including viewing the body, while others may stay in the lobby, lounge, or even just in the parking lot. Others may attend the funeral but not the wake.

Attending a funeral may be a new or frightening event for some students—possibly their first experience with cultural rituals surrounding death. To help them feel secure during this time, a familiar adult should be at the funeral home to support them if needed. If a family member is not available, someone from the school can be just as helpful. This support can range from simply being in the funeral home if you're needed to accompany the student into the room, to providing the security of touch by holding a student's hand, to putting your arm around a student, to just being a shoulder to cry on.

It would be helpful for the students if they were prepared beforehand as to what to expect at the funeral home and whether they should attend. They should also be informed about common funeral etiquette. When children know what to expect at a wake or funeral, they are better able to handle a difficult emotional experience. Find out beforehand as much as you can about the ceremonies (i.e., Will the casket be open? Will there be a religious service? Can the students attend as a group? Can special arrangements be made for the students?). Ask the funeral director to come to the school before the wake to talk with the students and answer any questions they may have.

If the family of the deceased student agrees, and the students are willing, it can be very meaningful for them to take some type of active role in the ceremonies, such as doing a reading or acting as pallbearers, ushers, or honor guard. Getting involved in this way provides a means of feeling useful at a time when it seems nothing can be done. It is usually comforting to the deceased student's family to have his classmates at the funeral.

☐ School Remembrance Activities

If the students are unable to attend the funeral, some substitute remembrance activity can be organized at the school. Remembering the deceased student through some form of school ceremony or observance can be a meaningful way for all interested students to become actively involved and feel as if they have contributed to honoring the memory of a friend.

This remembrance activity can be formal or informal, large or small, or short or long. It can involve the dead student's family or not. The choices of what to do are limited only by the creativity of those planning it and the financial or practical constraints of the school. One absolute must for the planning of this activity is to enlist student involvement. Students need the feelings of fulfillment and closure that come from organizing such an observance. Examples of remembrance activities include:

1. Tree or flower planting
2. Dedication of a plaque or picture
3. Fundraising for a scholarship or charity.
4. Purchase of a piece of equipment, relevant audio-visual materials, or books
5. Assembly of interested students, which can act as a memorial/remembrance service and can include:

   • Published readings
   • Stories or poems written by students and staff
   • Reflections on the life of the dead student
   • Music selected by students or some of the deceased's favorite music
   • Contribution by a member of the clergy familiar with the deceased student

- A collection of memorabilia that reflects the life of the student, including photos, pieces of his/her favorite sports equipment such as a tennis racquet, awards or trophies, artwork, or emblems of clubs or groups to which he belonged.

Prior to the remembrance service, students should be given information describing what will take place during the activity, possible emotional reactions, and proper etiquette during the service, as well as suggestions as to what to say to any of the deceased's family that may be present. Following the service, the students who attended should have an opportunity to gather together to discuss their feelings about the service and to have any questions answered that they may have.

Classes can either be cancelled or rearranged during the time that the interested students are attending the remembrance observance. This could also be a good time for the other students who did not attend to discuss among themselves and a teacher some aspect of life and death. Even though they may not have known the dead student, his death may have stimulated feelings of fear, apprehension, anxiety, or sadness that might be helpful for them to discuss.

It should be noted here that some schools have a policy of not conducting any type of special remembrance service or activity. The feeling is that once something is done for one deceased student, it must be done for all students who die, and there may be an instance where the school does not feel it is appropriate or necessary to do anything.

CHAPTER

Writing a Condolence Letter

One of the gestures of sympathy that can be done for a bereaved family is to send a condolence or sympathy note. Bereaved people have reported that these notes provide comfort and support for months or years following the death. The following suggestions about notes which are most comforting come from bereaved individuals:

- An informal letter or sympathy card with a personal note included seems to have the most meaning.
- Refer to the deceased by name whenever possible. Use the words "him" or "she" sparingly. Grieving families want to hear and see the name of their child or sibling.
- Start by stating how you heard about the death. For the survivors, this puts the death in the context of others' lives and gives a sense of sharing (Hasley, 1988).

  For example, "Yesterday I heard of Tim's death. I had just finished my last class of the day when Mrs. Thomas, the principal, called a special faculty meeting to inform us. All of us felt a sense of loss, and our hearts went out to you and your family."

- Share some of your memories about the deceased student. If he personally touched your life or others' lives, definitely share this.

  "Mary and I became friends when she was in my sixth grade class. She always had such a good sense of humor. If there was a group of students laughing, it was usually because Mary was telling some story in her unique way." Another example: "John was a student I will remember. His unique personality and his artistic ability made a special contribution to his class."

- Do not lie or falsely praise the student. Although all children are not outstanding students, everyone has something unique or positive to offer. Do not be afraid to write something humorous about the student. Even grieving people need laughter in their lives. For example, "I will miss Dave in class. The stories he would come up with for his lateness were so original; it was hard to be angry with him."
- If you offer assistance, be specific and follow through. Generally, offers such as, "If there is anything I can do, call me" are never acted on by bereaved families, because they do not want to impose. You could write, "I have some of Carrie's schoolwork I think you would like. I will bring it over next week." (Then be sure to take it to the family.) Or, "One of John's friends from last year moved away. I am sure he would want to know that John has died. I will notify him by phone and will give him your address."
- In ending the note, express your sorrow and offer some final words of support: "I am sorry Scott has died, and even though he will not be in our lives anymore, you can take pride in knowing he'll be in our thoughts and memories. I'll remember you and your family in my prayers."
- Do not be afraid to use the terms "dead," "died," or "death."
- Do not tell the family you know how they feel because you don't.
- Do not tell the family you know they will feel better soon because they may not.
- Do not mention that having other children must make it easier because it doesn't.
- Do not mention how hard it is to write the note or how inadequate you feel because this focuses on you, not the bereaved.

12
CHAPTER

When Death is by Suicide

The type of death in a school community that causes the most fear, con-fusion, guilt, and unanswered questions is death by suicide. Presently, suicide is the second leading cause of death among young people be-tween the ages of 15 and 24. The suicide rate for children ages 10 to 14 has doubled in the past 10 years (Parachin, 1998).

☐ Suicide Contagion

Some fear what is known as suicide contagion, where another person will copy the act of self-destruction. Although the incidence of suicide contagion is small, it should not be taken lightly. There have been some tragic examples in the past. Wrobleski (1995) explains, "A single study in 1986 received a tremendous amount of publicity. It claims that three fic-tionalized television programs about teenage suicide led to about eighty extra teenage suicides as a direct result of the dramas. Receiving no pub-licity were three other studies by other researchers who were unable to get the same results using the same methods.

"The original authors, in fact, tried and failed to repeat their results, and admitted in 1988 that 'the impact of the television broadcasts of fic-tional stories featuring suicidal behavior appears less widespread than we had originally proposed.' Even after strong evidence to the contrary, the belief is still widely held by experts and the public that teenage suicide is contagious" (p. 32).

This fear of clustering has caused some in the field of education to believe that a death by suicide should be treated differently from other types of death. They feel that the response described earlier in this book is only appropriate for a death other than a suicide. In the case of a suicide, they feel that an out-of-the-ordinary response should not be made. Nothing should be done to draw attention to the act or to glorify, honor, or condone it, so that others do not feel that they should imitate the act.

Frantz (1990), however, believes that a suicide death should be treated with the same procedure as a non-suicide death, maintaining that "There are instances of one suicide being followed by another, but it is extremely rare and is most likely to occur when a suicide is ignored and least likely to occur when a responsible, sensitive postvention program has been implemented."

When the death is a suicide, it is imperative that the school immediately seek the assistance of a trained member of a suicide support agency to field questions, talk with students and parents, and help the faculty identify other students who may require intervention at the time of the crisis (Cassini & Rogers, 1991).

☐ Response to Suicide

As with other types of death, the suicide of a member of the school community will elicit different responses from students and staff members. As explained in Chapter 2, there are a number of factors that affect a person's grief response. Three of the most common reactions, regardless of age, are fear, anger, and guilt.

Fear reactions are based on the possibility that other students may commit suicide or that they themselves might attempt a suicide. Anger is often directed at the deceased for purposely causing the emotional pain being experienced, and guilt can surface over why no one recognized that the person was suicidal.

Students at all levels need to be told the truth. Wrobleski (1994) believes this includes the very young: "Surely one shouldn't tell really young children? Perhaps not. Babies and two-year-olds need to understand that the person who died is gone permanently. Three and four-year-olds need to hear the truth simply, because if you do not tell them, they will find out, and it may be in an awful way. Obviously, little children do not need every single detail, but they need to know that the person did it to him or herself, and how, with a simple explanation of why. They need to know that some people feel so badly inside themselves that sometimes they kill themselves, because they cannot think of any other way of taking the hurt away. They need to know that people can be sick in their emotions as well as in their bodies" (p. 16).

Suicide should be defined to young children as the choice someone makes when deciding to make his body stop working. Age-appropriate facts and explanations should be given and myths about suicide should be dispelled. Adults should emphasize that suicide is a mistake because there is always another way (Goldman, 1994).

□ Warning Signs

Goldman (1994) warns that children may have suicidal thoughts but are afraid to express them. Sometimes children have suicidal thoughts and do express them, but no one listens or they are accused of being manipulative. Goldman also recommends that adults be aware of these signs of suicidal behavior following a suicide:

- Depressing thoughts and feelings
- Wishing to punish the person who died
- Wishing to die to relieve tremendous guilt
- Exhibiting self-anger and self-hatred
- Crying out for help
- Flirting with death
- Losing touch with reality
- Being preoccupied with one's own death
- Becoming socially isolated

□ Needs of Suicide Mourners

Regardless of age, those mourning a death by suicide have needs similar to those mourning another kind of death:

- To understand as much as possible
- To talk about the person and event
- Support from family and friends
- To express their emotions
- To look at guilt realistically
- To be reassured that their feelings are normal
- To memorialize the person's life

□ Helping Mourners of Suicide

These mourners can be helped through their grief by using the following suggestions:

- Let them talk about what they want when they want to
- Listen, reflect, clarify
- Give them permission to express any emotion
- Do not try to make them stop crying
- Help them piece facts together
- Don't try to move them along; let them lead
- Do not try to give answers
- Help them look at feelings realistically
- Encourage them to attend a support group
- Provide helpful literature
- Avoid simplistic explanations and cliches
- Use the name of the deceased

The following section of this chapter discusses a suicide prevention program for middle- and high-school students.

☐ Health Enhancement Through Asset Recognition: H.E.A.R. A School-Based Suicide Prevention Program

By Jane Emborsky, LPN, BS and Jenifer Lawrence, MS, CRC[1]

Adolescence is defined as the transitional period between childhood and adulthood. It is a time of tremendous change, as well as personal growth. It is a time when children begin to both pull away from the guidance and security of their family and venture out into the world to start to make decisions for themselves. Adolescence is a time of great ambivalence. On one hand, the child feels safe and secure when protected by the environment that the family, typically the parents, has created for them, but on the other hand, they also begin to resent the hold parents have on their very existence. Tension and increased stress levels are typical characteristics of the parent/adolescent interpersonal relationship.

Suicide among adolescents nationwide has been steadily and rapidly increasing over the past 30 to 40 years, with adolescent suicide rates more than tripling since 1960. Suicide is a leading cause of death for 15- to 24-year-olds, exceeded by only motor vehicle fatalities, and the sixth leading cause of death for 5- to 14-year-olds. The epidemic of adolescent suicide

---

[1]Jane Emborsky, LPN, BS is Director of Education, Information, and Self Help for the Mental Health Association in Niagara County, Inc., Lockport, New York.

Jenifer Lawrence, MS, CRC is Assistant Dean of the Graduate School of Education at the State University of New York at Buffalo, Amherst, New York.

takes on an even more dramatic dimension when the statistics of adolescent suicide attempts are factored in. According to a 1993 report issued by the National Center for Health Statistics, between 6 and 13 percent of all adolescents reported that they attempted suicide at least once in their lives, compared to a reported one percent in 1960. Roughly half of all adolescents in a typical high school class will report that they have, at one point in their life, thought of suicide. In fact, in an average American high school, approximately 3 percent of its students will attempt suicide each month.

To further complicate the issue, statistics on suicide are generally considered an underestimate of the true incidence. It is difficult to obtain accurate data on suicide because of the social stigma often attached to it. There is typically a tendency to underreport suicide because of reasons such as religious implications, concern for the family, or financial considerations regarding insurance payment restrictions. Therefore, many deaths actually due to suicide will be ultimately ruled as either accidental or undetermined.

Approximately 10 percent of suicide attempts will ultimately succeed. In fact, attempted suicide is one of the best predictors for identifying those adolescents most at risk for committing suicide. Although suicide was once thought of as an adult problem, it appears that the suicide rate is decreasing for all age groups except for adolescents. With this in mind, it is important to pay attention to several significant factors related specifically to adolescent suicide attempts.

Adolescent suicide is rarely precipitated by one single factor. There are, however, statistically significant factors or characteristics of adolescents who are more likely to attempt suicide. They are of limited value because none is a great predicator of suicide. We cannot take them too seriously, yet we have to take them seriously enough because they are the only things we have to go on.

A history of substance abuse, either drug or alcohol, makes a person vulnerable to suicidal ideations. While substance abuse does not cause an adolescent to commit suicide, it is an indicator that there is a problem. Use of alcohol or drugs can lower a person's inhibitions and increase the incidence of adolescent self-destructive behaviors.

If a family history of suicide exists, the odds go up that an adolescent will attempt suicide. There is still, to some extent, a taboo against suicide. Most adolescents grow up never thinking that they will attempt suicide or that any one of their family or friends will attempt suicide. When someone in their family breaks the taboo, it becomes easier for them to do it. The unthinkable has now become thinkable.

The United States has become the most transient nation in the world. It is not uncommon to meet adolescents who have moved four or five times during their lifetime. Moving, in itself, is a very stressful time in an adolescent's life. It typically requires leaving an accepting peer group, establishing and adjusting to new routines, and creating new identities in new environments. Thus, adolescents who move a lot are at a higher risk for suicide.

Loss of any kind may put an adolescent at risk for suicide. Frequent losses that occur in adolescence are loss through divorce, loss through death, loss through a relationship break-up, loss of friends, loss of extended family due to a move, and loss of a job and an expected standard of living.

Some adolescents are at risk when they face disappointments, such as social rejections, not making a sports team, or failing an exam. It is important to remember that it is not the severity of the adolescent's perceived problems that put them at risk, but their ability to cope with the problem. Those who cannot cope inevitably become emotionally vulnerable to suicide.

A history of depression makes one vulnerable to suicide, as a significantly high number of adolescents who die by suicide are depressed. Depressive symptoms in adolescence may include loss of interest in previously enjoyable activities and people, changes in eating and sleeping patterns, expressed feelings of helplessness and hopelessness, unusual neglect of personal appearance, or a preoccupation with death or suicide.

Adolescents who have been sexually or physically abused as children or young adults are at significant risk for suicide. Repeated acts of abuse destroy their sense of self-worth and self-esteem, often leaving them with feelings of guilt and helplessness.

Adolescence is an impulsive age, and suicide is an impulsive, self-destructive act. Adolescents with a history of self-destructive behavior, such as previous suicide attempts, self-mutilation, eating disorders, and substance abuse appear to be at greater risk than others.

Although one's initial reaction to this list of risk factors may be discouraging or disheartening, it is at least encouraging that many of these characteristics are sources of concern in and of themselves. They bring attention to the adolescent at risk. Therefore, the process by which we intervene for these reasons may indirectly reduce and prevent the likelihood of suicide.

In Support of H.E.A.R.

As statistics of adolescent suicide continue to rise, prevention has become a priority of many concerned professionals in the community. Mental health agencies, crisis hotlines, family physicians, clergy, law enforcement agents, and teachers are just some of the community resources available to help the adolescent.

To effectively address the issue of suicide prevention, coordinated and consultative efforts between the school and community need to be directed toward the general student population, not specifically those at risk. Because schools have an enormous amount of consistent and direct contact with a large population of adolescents, they are a strategic setting for the implementation of suicide prevention programs. To complement this resource, community mental health agencies have the knowledge, training, and expertise to work not only with the students themselves, but with the teachers and parents as well.

Working together to combine the educational expertise of the school with the interventional expertise of community mental health agencies, adolescents can greatly benefit by taking part in H.E.A.R., a suicide prevention curriculum designed to: 1) raise student awareness of the problem of adolescent suicide, as well as the clinical features associated with an adolescent who may be suicidal; 2) equip students with options for intervening in a potentially suicidal crisis; 3) reinforce the importance of establishing healthy coping mechanisms for the purpose of coping with the stresses of normal adolescent growth and development; 4) increase student awareness of self-esteem and the current societal influences that may potentially affect it; 5) introduce the concept of adolescent stress, stress management, and the value of support networks in alleviating stress; and 6) reinforce and work toward personal growth through building resiliency and recognizing already possessed assets.

H.E.A.R. is a school-based program that is a classroom-centered, knowledge-based, and student interactive model based on the assumption that the more students know about suicide warning signs, intervention strategies, and sources of help, the more likely they will be to ask for help or to refer peers for help. Classmates are often the first to notice suicidal ideations in their peers. In fact, the people most frequently approached by adolescents contemplating or planning suicide are their friends.

The goal of H.E.A.R. is to decrease the incidence of adolescent suicide by equipping and reinforcing students with the skills necessary to make a difference in the lives of their peers. In essence, the goal of H.E.A.R. is to empower students by improving their resiliency to cope with the everyday stresses of adolescence.

It is imperative that we as a community begin to address the needs of adolescents. Schools have this potential not only by training students to identify and help other students at risk for suicide, but by providing information that will help them understand and deal with their own feelings as well.

Session One: Education

GOAL 1: *To increase student awareness of potential risks, warning signs, and triggers of adolescent suicide*

Objectives:

1a: Present students with facts related to the incidence of adolescent suicide

1b: Present students with information regarding warning signs related to adolescent suicide

1c: Present students with information regarding trigger mechanisms related to adolescent suicide

1d. Present students with information regarding common myths related to adolescent suicide

Activities:

1. Discuss facts related to adolescent suicide
2. Discuss warning signs of suicide
3. Discuss trigger mechanisms
4. Discuss suicide myths

GOAL 2: *To enable students to identify suicidal ideations in their peers*

Objectives:

2a: Present students with examples of statements of adolescent suicidal ideations

2b: Present students with behaviors that may accompany adolescent suicidal ideations

2c: Present students with a case scenario

Activities:

1. Discuss examples of statements that may precede suicide
2. Discuss behaviors that may accompany suicidal ideations
3. Role-play case scenarios

GOAL 3: *To equip students with a plan of response when faced with a potentially suicidal peer.*

Objectives:

3a: Present students with suggestions for intervening in a potentially suicidal crisis

3b: Present students with steps to follow when they recognize the potential for suicide in a peer

Activities:

1. Discuss recognized interventions
2. Discuss suggested plan of response
3. Distribute crisis hotline number

GOAL 4: *To increase student awareness of the legal system as it applies to juvenile offenses.*

Objectives:

4a: Introduce students to a local law enforcement officer and representing agency

4b: Officer will present students with current facts and figures relating to local adolescent suicides following altercation with law enforcement, i.e., DWI, petty larceny, drug or weapon possession, assault

4c: Present students with options regarding due process of the law as it applies to juveniles

Activities:

1. Ask a local law enforcement officer and/or district attorney representative to present a 10 minute lecture to students regarding current statistics, due process, rehabilitation, and explanation of the 911 process.

Session Two: Coping Mechanisms

GOAL 1: *To increase student knowledge and awareness of characteristics displayed in suicidal adolescents*

Objectives:

1a: Present students with characteristic traits exhibited in adolescents who may be contemplating suicide

1b: Present students with types of problems and pain adolescents are frequently faced with

1c: Introduce students to the concept of levels of frustration tolerance

Activities:

1. Discuss character traits
2. Discuss types of problems
3. Discuss frustration tolerance scale

GOAL 2: *To increase student awareness of range and types of coping behavior*

Objectives:

2a: Define coping mechanism

2b: Present students with information regarding various coping styles common to adolescents

2c: Present students with information regarding how to discern healthy vs. unhealthy coping mechanisms and subsequent results

2d: Enable students to identify their own personal style of coping

Activities:
1. Discuss definition of coping mechanism
2. Discuss various coping styles
3. Discuss healthy vs. unhealthy coping mechanisms

GOAL 3: *To increase student awareness of the importance of maintaining connected with various sources of support*

Objectives:

3a: Define support system
3b: Identify potential supports commonly available to adolescents
3c: Present students with the concept of connectiveness and its importance in physical, emotional, and psychological well-being

Activities:
1. View and discuss available support systems
2. Brainstorm with students about potential sources of support that they are aware of at this time in their lives
3. Present students with two case scenarios illustrating opposing possibilities of the same situation

Session Three: Self-Esteem

GOAL 1: *To increase student awareness of the concept of self-esteem*

Objectives:

1a: Define self-esteem
1b: Present students with the ways self-esteem is influenced from birth to adolescence
1c: Present students with the concept of fluctuating self-esteem based upon environment, culture, and life events
1d: Introduce concept of global vs. personal self-esteem

Activities:
1. Discuss definition of self-esteem
2. Discuss various influences of self-esteem
3. Discuss fluctuations in self-esteem from birth to adolescence
4. Discuss and brainstorm with students the concept of global vs. personal self-esteem

GOAL 2: *To increase student awareness of current negative social influences upon adolescent behavior*

Objectives:

2a: Present students with information regarding the negative media influences, i.e., smoking, drinking, body image, sex, dress, cars

2b: Enable students to identify negative adolescent influences that lower self-esteem

2c: Present students with the concept of healthy vs. unhealthy expectations regarding normal life events, i.e., athletics, academics, popularity, material possessions

Activities:

1. Discuss negative media message influences
2. Facilitate sharing session of personal testimonies of deflation of self-esteem
3. Discuss healthy vs. unhealthy adolescent expectations

GOAL 3: *To increase student awareness of ways to improve self-esteem*

Objectives:

3a: Present students with the possibility that negative events can lead to positive outcomes

3b: Introduce students to the possibility that people can learn from this mistakes

3c: Introduce the concept of realistic goal setting in order to increase self-esteem

Activities:

1. Brainstorm ways negatives lead to positives
2. Offer students fill-in-the-blank scenarios with outcomes to choose from
3. Brainstorm scenarios to determine realistic goals

Session Four: Stress

GOAL 1: *To increase student knowledge and awareness of stress*

Objectives:

1a: Define stress and stress response

1b: Present students with the concept of healthy vs. unhealthy stress

1c: Present students with the characteristics of healthy vs. unhealthy stress

1d: Present students with short-term and long-term effects of stress on the body, i.e., physical, emotional, and psychological

Activities:

1. Discuss definition of stress
2. Discuss healthy vs. unhealthy stress
3. Brainstorm with students characteristics of healthy vs. unhealthy stress

GOAL 2: *To increase student awareness of how stress effects adolescents*

Objectives:

2a: Present students with stressors common to adolescents

2b: Present students with various common reactions exhibited by adolescents

2c: Present students with hypothesis that living with continued high levels of stress may lead to feelings of hopelessness, depression, and lack of control

2d: Present students with the idea that these feelings may lead to thoughts of suicide

Activities:

1. Discuss common adolescent stressors
2. Brainstorm common reactions to stress that can be observed in adolescents
3. Discuss consequences to high levels of stress

GOAL 3: *To increase student awareness of ways to decrease unhealthy stress*

Objectives:

3a: Present students with the concept and importance of stress release

3b: Present students with the concept of stress management

3c: Present students with activities to reduce stress

Activities:

1. Discuss methods of stress release
2. Discuss global use of stress management
3. View, discuss, and demonstrate various physical activities for immediate release of stress
4. View, discuss, and demonstrate various physical activities associated with long-term decrease of stress

Session Five: Personal Growth

GOAL 1: *To increase student awareness of the importance of offering and seeking support*

Objectives:

1a: Present students with positive and negative impacts of considering and seeking out these sources of support

1b: Present students with the possibility of including themselves as a possible source of support to their peers, as well as what may be involved, including both positive and negative ramifications

1c: Present student with options available to them when confronted by a suicidal peer, as well as the ramifications of each option

Activities:

1. Offer an interactive role-play involving suicidal ideations of a peer
2. Utilizing an open interactive forum, break into small groups for the purpose of discussing various sources of support available to adolescents; positive and negative impact of utilizing those supports; and

what is involved in becoming a source of support for another peer, including positive and negative ramifications

GOAL 2: *To increase student awareness that leadership qualities and characteristics will enable them to be looked upon as positive role models for their peers*

Objectives:

2a: Present students with characteristics of a positive leader

2b: Enable students to comprehend what it takes for them to be leaders

2c: Present to students that they have a choice in being a role model for their peers

Activities:

1. Discuss characteristics of a positive leader
2. Brainstorm what it takes to be a leader, including positives and negatives
3. Leadership activity

GOAL 3: *To increase student resilience to self-destructive behaviors, i.e., suicide, by promoting health enhancement through asset building*

Objectives:

3a: To assist students in acknowledging that they possess the skills and qualities that are needed to strengthen personal identities

3b: Define resiliency and explain how it can decrease attraction to risky behaviors

3c: Present students with the theory that resiliency/hardiness affects their ability to resist negative personal, societal, and environmental influences

3d: Provide students with an increased understanding that resiliency to negative influences will give them a sense of control over their lives

Activities:

1. Incorporating all of the objectives above for the purpose of combating negative adolescent influences, as well as demonstrating the importance of increasing self-esteem, losing inhibitions, and developing self-confidence within a team approach, the class will divide into small groups and participate in a group sculpture activity that involves interactive processing and positive evaluation from the entire class

☐ Factors Related to Adolescent Suicide

1. Roughly half of all adolescents in a typical high school class will report that they have, at one time in their lives, thought of suicide.
2. Women, in general, have a lower suicide rate than men, but a higher rate of attempt than men do.

3. Black females have the lowest suicide rate; black males have a lower suicide rate than white males.

4. Nine out of ten suicides occur in the home where the person lives; most suicides occur between 3 p.m. and midnight.

5. The months of the year with the highest suicide rates tend to be March and April. The months with the lowest suicide rates are August and January.

6. The most common method of suicide is by use of guns. The next common method is by hanging.

7. Adolescents who use and abuse drugs and alcohol have a higher suicide rate than those who don't.

8. Adolescents who are gay have a higher suicide rate than those who are straight.

9. Adolescents who have eating disorders have a higher suicide rate than adolescents who don't.

10. Adolescents who move a lot have a higher suicide rate than those who don't.

11. Adolescents who were sexually and/or physically abused as children or young adults have a higher suicide rate than those who weren't.

12. Adolescents who have been arrested have a higher suicide rate than those who have not.

13. Adolescents who have a multiple history of running away from home have a higher rate of suicide than those who do not.

14. Adolescents who live in an unstable home environment have a higher suicide rate than those who do not, i.e., living with an alcoholic or abusive parent.

15. Adolescents who have failed a grade or have been held back have a higher suicide rate than those who have not.

16. Adolescents who have attempted suicide once have a higher suicide rate than those who have not.

17. If there is a family history of suicide, the odds go up that the adolescent will attempt suicide as well.

18. In a school, once a suicide occurs in a given school year, the odds of another suicide occurring in that school year go up.

19. Adolescents who are suicidal often tell someone ahead of time that they are planning to kill themselves.

☐ Suicide Warning Signs

At least 75% of youth who commit suicide exhibit a series of common behaviors, which, if understood, become important clues to notice. Not all are seen in each case, so it is important to develop a sensitivity to the warning signals we may see and also be able to report these clues to others. If you suspect someone is thinking about suicide, watch the person, listen for messages, and look for these signs:

1. A previous suicide attempt, or the person has hurt him/herself on purpose (one of the strongest predicators for a completed attempt)
2. Personality changes or significant changes in behavior
3. Changes in eating patterns such as loss of appetite or excessive eating
4. Changes in sleeping patterns, such as insomnia or oversleeping, lasting for several days
5. Withdrawal from favorite activities
6. Breaking off completely from important relationships
7. A significant loss or failure, i.e., death of family member, break-up
8. Expressed feelings of helplessness, hopelessness, anxiety, guilt, and/ or difficulty concentrating
9. Suicidal thoughts, ideas, threats, or plans, especially if the plan is specific or lethal
10. Verbal comments that tell of plans to "end it all" or "I can't take it anymore"
11. Preoccupation with death or suicide, or themes of death or suicide in songs, movies, etc.
12. An increase in impulsive behavior such as beginning of risk-taking or self-destructive behavior
13. A change from depression to lightheartedness, sudden elation, or suddenly not talking about suicide anymore
14. A change in school attendance or a decline in grade performance
15. Giving away or disposing of prized possessions such as pictures, records, tapes, toys, or clothing
16. Evidence of alcohol or drug binges or other self-destructive behavior
17. Unusual neglect of personal appearance, putting oneself down, and self-criticism
18. Your "gut feeling" or intuition

☐ Common Trigger Mechanisms

The following is a list of trigger mechanisms associated with adolescent suicide. It is important to note that although they are often treated as the cause of suicide, they aren't. They are simply the trigger mechanisms that may lead a person to attempt to end his life.

1. Death of a family member or friend
2. The ending or break-up of a relationship
3. An instance of failure

4. Being arrested
5. An unexpected homosexual encounter
6. Becoming pregnant
7. Loss of a job or a coveted position (a role in a school play, starting on a basketball team, not chosen to be a camp counselor, etc.)

☐ Common Myths about Suicide

Myth #1: *People who talk about suicide are only trying to get attention. They really won't do it.*

Fact: Few people commit suicide without first letting someone else know how they feel. Those who are considering suicide give clues and warning signs as a cry for help. In fact, most seek out someone to rescue them. Over 70% of those who threaten to commit suicide either make an attempt or complete the act.

Myth #2: *Talking about suicide will make it happen.*

Fact: Wrong, wrong, wrong. Talking about suicide doesn't place ideas in people's heads that were not already there. Discussing it openly helps the suicidal person sort through the problems and generally provides a sense of relief and understanding. It is one of the most helpful things you can do.

Myth #3: *People who commit suicide don't warn others.*

Fact: Out of ten people who kill themselves, eight have given definite clues to their intentions. They leave numerous clues and warnings to others, although some of their clues may be non-verbal or difficult to detect.

Myth #4: *There is a certain type of person who commits suicide.*

Fact: There is no type—young, old, rich, poor, popular, unpopular, athletic, good student, bad student, and so on.

Myth #5: *Once a person decides to commit suicide, there is no way of stopping him/her.*

Fact: Most of the time, a suicidal person is ambivalent about the decision; he is torn between wanting to die and wanting to live. Most suicidal people don't want to die—they just want the pain to stop.

Myth #6: *After a person has attempted suicide, it is unlikely they will try again.*

Fact: People who have attempted suicide are very likely to try again. 80% of people who commit suicide have made at least one previous attempt.

Myth #7: *Only people who are mentally ill commit suicide.*

Fact: Those who attempt or complete suicide may be overwhelmingly depressed and hopeless, but they have not necessarily lost touch with reality.

Myth #8: *An unsuccessful attempt means that the person wasn't serious about ending his life.*

Fact: The attempt in and of itself is the most important factor; not the method.

☐ Suicide Interventions

Do These Things in an Immediate Crisis:

- *Remain calm.* Stay with the person. Show him that you care.
- *Get vital information.* If you do not know the person, get his name, address, phone number, and the name(s) of his parent(s).
- *Get help.* Send someone to get an adult (parent, teacher, coach) or dial 911.
- *Assure the person that he or she has done the right thing by talking to you.*
- *Get the person to talk.* Talk directly about the suicide. Discussing the suicide or asking the person if he has a specific plan will allow you to assess the urgency of the situation.
- *Establish eye contact and speak in a calm, low voice.*
- *Try to get the person to agree to a verbal "No Suicide" Contract.* The contract reads, among other things, "No matter what happens, I will not kill myself."
- *Wait until help arrives.* Do not leave until a responsible adult is with the suicidal person.
- *Allow yourself the opportunity to talk about the suicide intervention with a trusted adult.*

Do Not Do These Things:

- Do not ignore your intuitions if suicide is suspected.
- Do not minimize the person's threat. Take it seriously.
- Do not be concerned about long periods of silence. Give the person time to think.
- Do not leave the person. Do not let him/her go to the restroom.
- Do not lose patience with the person.
- Do not argue with the person about whether suicide is right or wrong.
- Do not promise confidentiality. Instead, promise help and privacy.
- Do not discuss the incident with others. This includes peers or friends, but it is okay to discuss it with a trusted adult.

☐ How You Can Help in a Suicidal Crisis

- *Recognize the clues to suicide.* Look for symptoms of deep depression and signs of hopelessness and helplessness. Listen for suicide threats and words of warning, such as "I wish I were dead," or "I have nothing to live for." Watch for despairing actions and signals of loneliness; notice whether the person becomes withdrawn and isolated from others. Be alert to suicidal thoughts as depression lifts.

- *Trust your own judgment.* If you believe someone is in danger of suicide, act on your beliefs. Don't let others mislead you into ignoring suicidal signals.
- *Tell others.* As quickly as possible, share your knowledge with parents, friends, teachers, or other people who might help in a suicidal crisis. Don't worry about breaking a confidence if someone reveals suicidal plans to you. You may have to betray a secret to save a life.
- *Stay with a suicidal person.* Don't leave a suicidal person alone if you think there is immediate danger. Stay with the person until help arrives or a crisis passes.
- *Listen intelligently.* Encourage a suicidal person to talk to you. Don't give false assurances that "everything will be okay." Listen and sympathize with what the person says. Try to stay calm and be as understanding as possible.
- *Urge professional help.* Strongly suggest that the suicidal person seek help from a psychiatrist, psychologist, social worker, counselor, or other professional during a suicidal crisis or after a suicide attempt. Encourage the person to continue with therapy even when it seems difficult.
- *Know the resources in advance.* Becoming educated regarding the people and agencies in your community you can turn to in a suicidal crisis can save a lot of time and stress should the need for these services arise. Your ability to calmly provide these resources to a friend may provide hope.

☐ What Do You Say?

Imagine yourself in a situation which might make you wonder if life were worth continuing. Not a fatal illness or injury, but something so emotionally painful that suicide might seem like one way to stop the pain. This might include losing someone through rejection, separation, or death; failing at something important; doing something you can't forgive yourself for; or feeling paralyzed by depression and afraid that you'll never get better.

Now imagine yourself alone, thinking, "I don't have to suffer like this. I can end it all right now." You are terrified that you'll act on this feeling. You have pills handy, or maybe a gun. It all seems so easy. Instead, you reach for the phone and call someone—a friend, someone in your family, a stranger, maybe a hotline...

☐ What Would You *Want* From That Person? What *Wouldn't* You Want?

This is what most people would want:

- Someone who has time to listen to *them*
- A calm voice
- Assurance that they're not crazy
- To be taken seriously
- To feel loved
- Someone to be there
- To feel important to another person
- To be believed without having to prove anything
- To have someone on their side
- To feel safe
- To be held
- Respect
- Undivided attention
- To be understood
- Someone who won't hold it against them later
- To be in charge of what happens to them
- Someone to come over
- To be put at ease
- Hope
- Relief
- To be taken care of
- To feel they could trust the person
- Someone to say "I care about you"
- To be accepted as they are
- To keep their dignity

Most people would not want:

- To be told it's wrong or silly to feel this way
- Pity
- Rejection
- To be alone
- To feel embarrassed for having called
- A lecture or a sermon
- A pep talk
- A debate

- A scolding (You're stronger than that.")
- The third degree—to be pumped for information
- False reassurances ("It will be better in the morning")
- Clichés
- To be put down
- To be let down
- To be criticized
- To be analyzed
- To be categorized
- To be told what to do—advice unasked for
- To be lied to
- To be tricked
- To be interrupted
- A guilt trip
- Comparisons—to be one-upped by someone worse off than they are
- To be put on the defensive
- To be patronized
- Phoniness
- To have someone try to cheer them up
- Panic
- To feel like a burden
- To have someone try to change the subject
- To be put on "hold"
- To be referred
- To be treated like a "case"

13

CHAPTER   Patricia L. Evans

Coping and Healing:
The Aftermath of Violence
and Murder

People never want to believe that the murder of innocent people will occur at the school in their community, or worse, at the school where they work or have a child in attendance. Yet the news tells us that this is an all too great possibility. Between February 1997 and June 1998 there were shootings at six schools throughout the United States, resulting in 17 deaths and a multitude of injuries. In April 1999, shootings at schools in Taber, Alberta, Canada and Littleton, Colorado left 14 dead. These figures reflect only those incidents caused by students, and do not take into account situations where the perpetrator was a trespasser on school property. They also do not include incidents where students have randomly shot and killed teachers and classmates at school-related functions held off campus, such as the May 1998 incident in Edinboro, Pennsylvania.

Shootings have occurred mostly in small communities in Alaska and in the southern, northwestern, and eastern regions of the contiguous United States (Eagen, 1998). Old stereotypes of violence erupting only in inner-city schools, related to drugs and gang warfare, are clearly shattered. New concerns have been brought to the forefront, and the need for all schools to have in place a comprehensive crisis plan complete with short- and long-term strategies is underscored. The odds of any given school encountering this type of violence are statistically small; however, experience tells us it could happen anywhere.

☐ A Few Words About Prevention

Although violence prevention is not the focus of this chapter, efforts to prevent such an event from occurring should be of prime concern in all communities. Resources for developing and implementing preventive measures prior to a crisis are available through the following organizations as listed in Appendix A:

* Anti-Violence Partnership (AVP) of Philadelphia
* National Organization for Victim's Assistance (NOVA)
* Center for the Prevention of School Violence
* National Association of State Boards of Education Publications

An effective Crisis Response Plan with multiple interventions including follow-up and referral mechanisms also offers the potential to prevent future violence. Part of the training for administrators, teachers, staff, parents, and others that will comprise the Crisis Response Team should include basic information regarding trauma, loss, and the impact these factors have on individuals. Team members, therefore, are given the opportunity to better detect symptomatic behavior, make referrals, and gain a greater understanding of the needs of children who experience losses, violence, and/or other trauma in their personal lives.

There is a growing body of literature suggesting that effective treatment of traumatic exposure is important in the prevention of ongoing violence (Nader, 1997a, 1997c; Newberger & Newberger, 1992; Wilson & Raphael, 1993). Unresolved trauma and traumatic grief have been shown to be a factor for a number of individuals who inflict violence on others (Duncan, 1958; Ressler & Burgess, 1985; van der Kolk, 1989). Examples come from the psychological histories of the sniper who opened fire on an elementary school playground in Los Angeles and from a woman who shot herself in front of a classroom of fifth graders after having held them hostage (Nader, 1997c). An increase in individual and family violence was observed in the aftermath of the 1993 mid-western floods (Kohly, 1994). The 13 year-old involved in the Arkansas school shooting that left four dead is reported to have been the victim of sexual abuse (*New York Times*, 1998).

☐ The Necessity of Outside Professionals

Catastrophic events can affect an entire community as well as an entire school. Developing linkages with various community agencies and organizations whose help may be drawn upon in the time of crisis is an essential component to the plan (Ritter, 1994). Utilization of outside personnel, as discussed in an earlier chapter, is an important inclusion to the school's own Crisis Intervention Team. In some school districts, administrators and others believe that all loss and death situations are best handled by the psychologists, social workers, and others on staff. For example, following the Paducah, Kentucky, school shooting in which three were killed, a crisis team from the National Organization for Victim's Assistance (NOVA) was called in by a county judge to provide interventions primarily for the community. The school was said to have had its own initial interventions. While there, the NOVA team offered additional help for the school. Initially, school leaders were reluctant to make use of the outside assistance. The principal, however, agreed that the NOVA team's help was needed, once it was realized that no debriefing had taken place to help faculty deal with the violent death and injury of several students. After the intervention, the principal told his faculty that while he previously did not see the need for this type of assistance, he thought differently now and, in fact, wanted more services from the NOVA team while still in Paducah (Poland, 1998a).

When a school experiences multiple deaths and injuries, administrators, teachers, staff, students, and their families will all be traumatized by the incident. According to the fourth edition of the Diagnostic and Statistical Manual of Mental Disorders (DSM-IV) (American Psychiatric Association, 1994), events that are likely to elicit post-traumatic stress responses, including the risk of post-traumatic stress disorder (PTSD), include but are not limited to those in which an individual:

- Experiences actual or threatened serious harm
- Witnesses the death, serious injury, or a threat to the physical integrity of another person
- Learns about the violent death, serious harm, or threat of death or serious injury to a loved one or close associate

From a thanatological perspective, Therese Rando (1993) indicates that factors which make any death circumstance traumatic and thereby increase the risk of complicated grief include:

- Suddenness and lack of anticipation
- Violence, mutilation, and destruction
- Preventability and/or randomness
- Loss of a child
- Multiple deaths

Redmond (1989) tells us that murder, more than any other type of death, affects a larger circle of people. To one degree or another, then, the entire school community and their family members will be experiencing traumatic and/or grief reactions following a murder. As Deborah Spungen

(1998) points out, most of these people are wounded emotionally, spiritually, and psychologically by the murders, some more deeply than others. Those at the scene of the violence and murder are the victims. Others whose lives are deeply affected as a result of the incident are its co-victims.

How well children and adolescents adjust to and recover from the trauma and consequent losses will be determined, in part, by the degree of ongoing distress experienced by adults responsible for their care. Adult post-traumatic reactions affect the quality of support and assistance given to children and have the potential to cause secondary harmful effects. Further, the degree to which school personnel are able to return the school to pre-trauma levels of functioning is contingent upon the amount of distress they are experiencing (Nader & Pynoos, 1993; Stevenson, 1994).

Outside sources of assistance and referral can be accessed through local hospices, hospitals, American Red Cross, mental health and related human services agencies, local colleges or universities, and victim advocacy agencies or groups. Depending on the particular state or locale, victim advocates may be located through police departments, sheriff departments, or the district attorney's office. Resources at the national level include the National Organization for Victim's Assistance (NOVA) and International Critical Incident Stress Foundation (ICISF).

NOVA and ICISF each have provided information, personnel, and other services following a number of catastrophic events including the Dahmer case in Minneapolis, the Oklahoma City bombing, various natural disasters, and recent school shootings. Both organizations will send a national crisis team to the site of the trauma under certain conditions as discussed below.

NOVA will supply a national Crisis Response Team, upon request only, for a three- to four-day time period, and for the following specific purposes:

- To identify those most affected by the tragedy (e.g., victims and their families, classmates, and teachers)
- To provide support and training to local counselors, psychologists, and other caregivers
- To conduct an open forum for the community to process feelings about the tragedy (Poland, 1998b)

Additional support or assistance is provided as needed (e.g., assistance with counseling and debriefing) when the team is on site. Once the team has left an area, NOVA remains available as a resource to the community. The NOVA team that went to Paducah, Kentucky, was asked to come by a county judge. Another team went to Jonesboro, Arkansas, following the March 24, 1998 school shooting. This team was requested by the Arkansas Attorney General and the county prosecutor. It consisted of two local psychologists, three victims advocates, a minister, and a police lieutenant (Poland, 1998b). Since it was contacted almost immediately, the team arrived in Jonesboro within 26 hours of the shooting.

The International Critical Incident Stress Foundation was founded with the purpose of providing debriefing for frontline emergency personnel, such as emergency medical teams, firefighters, etc. While this remains the primary focus of the foundation's services, it has expanded its role. The ICISF maintains a 24-hour hotline and puts communities experiencing an emergency in touch with the nearest Critical Incident Management Team(s). Over 400 teams from throughout the United States are registered with the Foundation. Should a nearby team not be available, the Foundation will get in touch with and send a team(s) from another locale.

When the emergency is of significant size and requiring more assistance, ICISF will assemble and send a national Crisis Intervention Management team – usually within a 24-hour time frame. Professionals with expertise in specific areas (e.g., a bereavement and trauma specialist for adolescents) can be similarly accessed through the foundation. NOVA and ICISF maintain a working relationship with one another. Both have gone to the same site of a tragedy and worked in complementary roles. It should be emphasized, however, that use of either of these or similar organizations does not preclude the necessity for a school to have its own Crisis Response Plan.

☐ Responding to Trauma and Grief

If recovery and healing of the school milieu is to occur, it is essential that personnel involved with psychological first aid, interventions, and postventions include those who have knowledge of grief and traumatology. Referrals for counseling or therapy should be made to professionals with training or credentials as bereavement and trauma specialists.

Many helpers at the site of a violent trauma, especially one involving children, report being unprepared for the intensity of survivors' reactions. When children, adolescents, or adults encounter traumatic loss, they experience both traumatic reactions and grief, plus the interplay of the two (Doka, 1996; Figley, Bride, & Mazza, 1997; Hendriks, Black, & Kaplan, 1993; Rando, 1993; Raphael, 1986; Redmond, 1989; Wilson & Raphael, 1993). Simpson (1997, p. 6) asserts, "You may have grief without much trauma, but you can never have much trauma without grief. Ignoring the trauma component of grief or the grief component of trauma is surely negligent."

In many cases, attention will need to focus on the effects of the trauma prior to those associated with grieving. The sooner victims and co-victims, regardless of age, are able to talk about and process what happened to them and their reactions, the better (e.g., within a 24-hour time frame). Post-trauma stress can be like a blanket covering the grief, and it thereby inhibits its expression, ultimately delaying or preventing long-term adaptation to the loss (Rando, 1993). Mere facilitation of grief will be insufficient and potentially anti-therapeutic for those bereaved through trauma.

Unrecognized, unacknowledged, and/or inappropriately treated trauma and grief responses have the potential to cause problems in children's development and interfere with school performance. Long-term effects may include irritability, bullying and other forms of aggression, memory and concentration problems, substance abuse, promiscuity, and various mental health disturbances such as anxiety and mood disorders (Eth & Pynoos, 1985; Garbarino, Kostelny, & Dubrow, 1991; Nader, Pynoos, Fairbanks, & Fredricks, 1990; Rando, 1993; Terr, 1991; van der Kolk & Saporta, 1991).

☐ An Overview of Reactions

A comparison of grief and trauma reactions shows striking similarities and important differences. In general, the combination of trauma and bereavement intensifies and may prolong symptoms common to both. Grief should be viewed as a normal adjustment and healing process to loss. Traumatic responses also involve a process towards adaptation. The interplay of trauma and grief reactions to violence is normal responses to an abnormal event (McCann & Pearlman, 1990).

When someone is confronted with a major loss such as the death of a loved one, some cognitive dissonance is usually experienced. Even when a death has been expected, its irreversibility and finality are difficult to reconcile. The mystery of life and death is so poignant; that is, how someone can be living one moment, no matter how tenuously or belabored the breathing, and the next moment he is no longer alive and never, ever will be again (at least not in the same way or form, depending on religious beliefs).

Disbelief and some denial are usual to the grief process. When the death or other major loss occurs swiftly without warning, there is an inability to comprehend the reality. Individuals are thrown into an essential conflict between the world the way it was, the way they dreamed or hoped it might become, and the way it suddenly is. Responses such as, "Oh, my God, no," "It isn't true," or "There's some mistake" are common. When violent death or injury caused through the willful intent of another human being is involved, the shock and denial are even further intensified.

Nothing makes sense as the mind struggles to comprehend the incomprehensible. Witnesses and victims of the violence may be so dazed and shocked that they retreat into themselves, numbed beyond feeling.

Others, including family members of the traumatized and dead, will want and demand information as they try desperately to make sense of it all. Questions about the circumstances leading up to, during, and immediately following the attack will be asked over and over. No answer at this point satisfies sufficiently, no matter how factual or accurate. The most difficult question, and the one most often asked is the unanswerable "Why?" In the days following 15-year-old Kipland Kindel's shooting rampage at Thurston High School in Springfield, Oregon, a sign was erected at the site where two students died that simply read, "Why, Kip?" (Eagen, 1998).

Anger is a normative reaction to loss and is common to both grief and trauma. Anger following trauma, especially violent death at the hands of another human, is intensified generally to the point of rage. The intensity of these feelings is especially difficult for others to comprehend. Some people will experience anger and rage immediately. In part, anger mobilizes energy in the face of feeling helpless and out of control. It also acts as a defense against deep, searing psychic pain caused by the senseless murder of a loved one.

Survivors often displace their anger. Children may be angry with parents, teachers, and other adults for not protecting them. Anger coupled with the search for "why" can fuel concerns about who is to blame. Scapegoating, hurtful accusations, and inappropriate litigation are but a few of the potential negative results that need to be guarded against (Nader & Pynoos, 1993). Self-control is lower than usual, and an individual's ability to tolerate even minor irritations will be compromised. This is particularly true of and difficult for children whose coping mechanisms are naturally immature, and for adolescents who are developmentally at the point of heightened emotionality.

There is also an intense need for justice. Fantasizing ways to get revenge for the terrible injustice done to them and/or others is common for survivors (Redmond, 1989). For example, this author fantasized about pushing the person convicted of shooting her son out of a plane over the middle of Iceland in January and leaving him for dead in a desolate area. In a teen support group, the brother of a murder victim said he had thoughts of shooting the assailant in the stomach and kneecaps, then leaving him to die in agony in the desert. These feelings and thoughts can be frightening and may generate a sense of shame by those holding them. They are normal responses and do not make the person feeling them "bad" (Spungen, 1998). Taking action on them, however, becomes violent behavior which must be prevented.

In at least two of the school shootings during the 1997-98 school year, the young assailants expressed retaliatory wishes because of their own previous victimization. Luke Woodham, convicted of killing three people in Mississippi, wrote in his journal, "I do this to show society, 'Push us and we will push back' . . . I suffered all my life. No one ever truly loved me." One of his victims was his mother (Eagen, 1998). Thirteen-year-old Mitchell Johnson, one of two youngsters accused of killing five people at a school in Jonesboro, Arkansas, is reported to have wanted to "get even" because of being sexually abused.

Encouraging the safe expression of anger and retaliation fantasies can help to defuse them. As Redmond (1989) states, "It is in venting and verbalizing the murderous impulses that the anger begins to lose some of its intensity and power" (p. 33). Eventually, the energies generated through the anger can be transformed into constructive rather than destructive ends. This, in fact, should be one of the goals of intervention—to assist survivors and the community to use anger and rage as a mobilizer for positive action (Nader & Pynoos, 1993). Energies might be used towards prevention and/or recovery efforts for one another, the school, and the community. Students Against Drunk Driving, Families of Murder Victims, and the National Victim Center are but three examples of organizations whose origins involved the transformation of angry energies (see Appendix A).

Rechanneling energies in the above ways is healthy for those affected by the trauma, and it can ultimately give meaning to the loss(es). Attempts to positively direct anger and rage, however, are not likely to be successful until there has been an opportunity to first safely vent and verbalize (Redmond, 1989). Debriefing sessions can provide such an opportunity. Holding meetings for various groups (e.g., students, parents, faculty and staff, general community) has been shown to be useful (Poland, 1998). Making the school gym available and encouraging students to participate in physical activities can be beneficial in defusing some of their anger and frustrations.

Any major loss also carries with it a loss of trust, predictability, and security. Fear and apprehension are common to both traumatic losses and those of a less catastrophic nature. Violent traumatic events, though, generate excessive fear, and in some, panic. All individuals at the school on the day of the violence will have been terrorized. One school psychologist writes of his experience at the Jonesboro, Arkansas, school shootings: "There was a *total* terror everywhere! I served two tours in Vietnam and I had total flashback to that time" (Gorin, 1998).

Trauma survivors of all ages report feelings of great vulnerability. There are both new fears and intensification of old ones (Nader & Pynoos, 1993; Redmond, 1989; Spungen, 1998; Terr, 1991). The world is no longer as safe a place as it seemed before the event. Beliefs and assumptions about personal invulnerability, the good will be protected, children don't kill, violent and horrible events happen at other schools—in other communities—to other people, etc. are all shattered. Survivors feel betrayed and violated. Hypervigilance can be a frequent result as individuals fear for their own safety and that of others. Parents, teachers, and other adults may become overprotective of children, sometimes to the point of inhibiting normal development. Commonly, traumatized adults as well as children will experience an exaggerated startle response to loud noises or any unusual, unexpected sound or sight (American Psychiatric Association, 1994; Rando, 1993).

Intervention strategies must be directed at restoring a sense of safety and normalcy. Like other feelings associated with the trauma and grief, fear needs to be acknowledged, openly expressed, and examined for its orientation to reality. Support groups can be helpful in this regard. Resuming classes as soon as it is reasonable and possible provides for a much-needed sense of routine and continuity amid much chaos and change. Safety measures can be instituted according to the particular situation and school needs. This may mean adding security personnel or police to the school grounds and buses, organizing a buddy system for walking home, increasing hall monitors, etc. (Goldman, 1996).

Preoccupation with thoughts of the loss and some re-experiencing of that loss have been long recognized as part of the grief process (Freud, 1917; Lindemann, 1944). This generally takes the form of a deep yearning, longing for, and reminiscing about the loved one. The need to talk about the loved one may be strong for many bereaved. Remembering is bittersweet. It can be pleasurable as well as sad. Remembering also helps to confirm the reality of the death and to eventually integrate the death into the sum total of the grieving person's life experiences.

When violent trauma is involved, re-experiencing occurs through intrusive and distressing thoughts, images and, often, nightmares. As such, there is a reliving of the helplessness, terror, and horror of the event. Individuals of all ages have a need to tell and retell their story and the details of the trauma. There is a desperate need to make sense of what happened, to verify that it's reality. While serving a similar purpose as grief memories, traumatic memories can be overwhelming and may interfere with the necessary working through of grief reactions.

Affected persons, most especially children, are likely to need assistance to process them (Nader, 1997b). Inability to process the memories keeps the event and feelings associated with it in the here and now. The survivor continues to live the traumatic occurrence. It is prevented from becoming an integrated part of the person's past. As Bagge and Brandsma (1994) state, "The more foreign the new experience is to the individual's previous experiences, the greater the difficulty in the information acquiring a sense of 'then and there' or being processed and stored in the relatively affect-free database (historical memory)" (p. 577).

Offering opportunities for victims and co-victims to express their reactions, to tell their stories soon after (e.g., within 24 hours) the trauma facilitates processing and integration of the experience. This is true for children and adolescents as well as adults (Wilson & Keane, 1997). Interventions directed at encouraging processing for students might include:

- Holding open meetings for different age groups at which a school psychologist, social worker, or other counselor is present to guide the process
- Offering 24-hour counseling services for the first day or two immediately following the violence
- Making individual counseling available
- Encouraging peer support groups and providing a designated space for them
- Providing counselors on buses the day that school resumes following the incident
- Having counselors in every classroom at the beginning of the day when classes resume with special attention focused on classrooms from which a teacher or students were killed

These interventions can be modified to meet the needs of the particular school, the severity of the violence and death, and the amount of counseling help available. Westside Middle School in Arkansas was able to amass a cadre of 150 caregivers who counseled approximately 1,000 students and parents in a 24-hour period (Gorin, 1998).

Children are known to use play to express and work through their reactions. This will be true of both grief and trauma and is related to the re-experiencing of the event. Traumatic play, however, is likely to be considerably more distressing for the child and may be misunderstood by adults. For children who witnessed the violence, reenacting it over and over through play and related means (e.g., artwork, music) allows them to take it outside of themselves and to separate the act of violence from their friends, teachers, and/or loved ones who were involved (Goldman, 1996). Children who were not at the site of the violence may also use play as a means of expressing their reactions. This can be an important way for adults to learn what these children believe happened versus what actually occurred. What youngsters imagine took place may be more frightening than the reality.

It is difficult to experience any major loss, much less the death or serious injury of children, without some feelings of guilt. The educational system teaches us to look for cause and effect. In the search for a reason, the "if only" and "I should have . . . " thoughts loom before us. We assume responsibility and ascribe guilt to self. Guilt and responsibility may weigh heavily on school faculty, administrators, and staff who feel they were unable to sufficiently protect children in their care.

There will be some who, in hindsight, believe they should have seen warning signs. Many who were at the site of the violence will feel guilty because they survived while some of the students and/or co-workers did not. This is analogous to the survivor guilt soldiers experience when their buddies die in battle and they do not. Guilt can serve to counter some of the feelings of helplessness and is often irrational following traumatic events. Children are especially vulnerable to feeling a sense of responsibility and guilt, but they are the most overlooked in this regard.

Loneliness and a sense of emotional isolation occur following both the death of a loved one and a traumatic experience. The death of someone to whom we have formed an attachment always leaves a void. When individuals are bereaved due to a violent death, these feelings are likely to be profound. Others may have little patience or understanding for the grieving process, much less the intensity of traumatic reactions. Individuals less affected by the trauma, or who recover at a relatively quick rate, may become impatient with the continuing pain of their friends, co-workers, and family. The way the death occurred may be threatening to others who can no longer deny that such a thing could also happen in their lives, to their loved ones. Consequently, the bereaved are avoided. The traumatized griever feels like a social outcast and is, thus, disenfranchised (Doka, 1988; Spungen, 1998).

Feelings of being stigmatized can affect the entire school, even the entire community as nationwide, and perhaps worldwide, as media focuses on the tragedy. In the aftermath of a shooting that left four dead and twenty-two injured, a message on a theater marquee in Springfield, Oregon, read, "We have done nothing wrong" (Eagen, 1998).

Grief Triggers

The bereaved describe experiencing episodes of grief that are like waves washing over them, often when they least expect it. These episodes are generally in response to some reminder—tangible and intangible—of the person and the relationship they loved. Many survivors and co-victims of trauma continue to re-experience aspects of the event over a lengthy period of time. These are usually triggered by something that symbolizes or resembles the traumatic event. Triggers will be different for different people. Redmond (1989) lists these triggers:

- Anniversaries of the trauma
- Holidays (e.g., Christmas)
- The beginning of the next school year or semester
- Media articles, movies, television shows about a similar event
- Music
- Criminal justice proceedings
- Sensing, in which individuals may hear, smell, see, hear, touch, or taste something similar to an aspect of the traumatic event (e.g., the smell of pines if the violence took place near pine trees; the sound of sirens, etc.).

Strategies can be devised to minimize some of the effect of certain triggers, such as developing plans for anniversary and holiday reactions. Local hospices and mental health organizations, the National Hospice Organization, Association for Death Education and Counseling (ADEC), and NOVA (see Appendix A) can assist in this type of planning.

Criminal justice proceedings, especially a trial, can be highly distressing for victims and co-victims. Some individuals will be called upon to testify as witnesses. Media attention will once again focus on the events of the trauma as well as on the trial. The school and the community may feel that they are the ones on trial. Considerable reliving of the horror of the killings and a reexperiencing of traumatic grief reactions is to be expected during this time. Strong reactions may persist in the days immediately following the trial (Spungen, 1998). There may be temporary elation (if justice is perceived to be served) that soon turns to sadness, anger, and grief. For some, the grieving process may only now begin.

When the perception is that the trial and/or the verdict were unjust, the depth of the anger, pain, and possibly depression can be almost unimaginable. During the trial and the days immediately following, it will be helpful to:

- Provide relevant information
- Encourage the use of victim advocate services, especially for those serving as witnesses, those injured during the violence, and the bereaved family
- Offer peer support groups and individual counseling
- Have a plan for dealing with the media
- Recognize that some faculty or staff may need time off or extra assistance

Second Wounds

Following a violent trauma, victims and many co-victims are in a state of emotional dependency, trusting that others will give support and assistance in coping with the event, remedying injustices, and so on. All too often, they are "injured" a second time by the insensitivity, lack of understanding and/or ignorance of those around them (Redmond, 1989; Spungen, 1998).

For example, at a bereavement support group, one mother told others that as soon as she learned that her teenage son had been killed by a drunk driver, she rushed to the hospital where he had been taken. Upon finding the doctor, she inquired as to where her son was and if she could see him to say goodbye. The doctor told her, "The body has been...." She didn't hear anymore as the cold, impersonal words "the body" imprinted themselves on her mind. Her sense of shock was intensified. She said she was unable to respond at the time, but wanted to scream, "That is my Jimmy, my child, my baby."

A young man who had been shot after having been abducted and held hostage for several hours told of being asked by a baseball coach if the perpetrator was bigger than he. The implication was that the boy could have prevented much of what happened to him and that therefore, he bore some responsibility. This is similar to rape victims who are made to feel they "asked for it" because of what they were wearing when the rape occurred.

Second wounds contribute to the stigmatization and social isolation discussed previously, and they compound the healing process. Sources of second wounds may come from anywhere which include:

- Medical and health care personnel
- The criminal justice system
- The media
- Mental health and related human services personnel
- Social service workers
- Clergy
- Family, friends, and co-workers
- Educators, school administrators, and counselors

Assessment of Children's Symptoms

As noted earlier, several groups of people are at risk for troubling symptoms and long-term negative effects following a violent trauma resulting in the death and injury of many individuals. Children and adolescents, especially those injured or otherwise having witnessed the violence, are at high risk. Accurate assessment that leads to effective treatment can go a long way towards preventing or minimizing PTSD and an array of social, behavioral, and mental health problems, including acts of violence

(Nader, 1997c). While many of the interventions directed at psychological first aid will minimize the severity of reactions, some students may continue to experience effects that are troubling. Strategies for assessment should be included in a comprehensive Crisis Response Plan. Ideally, assessment information on children and adolescents should come from clinicians, teachers, and parents.

An array of valid assessment instruments are available for children as young as three through adolescence. Best results have been obtained when a trained clinician, such as the school psychologist, administers these assessments. When they should be given will vary depending on the particular child, instrument, and/or situation (Wilson & Keane, 1997). Three to five weeks following the incident is most often recommended.

Parents, other family members (e.g., grandparents), and teachers have the potential to be the best detectors and reporters of symptoms in children. Their own degree of distress, however, may affect reporting. Traumatized teachers or those who feel considerable guilt may underreport changes in children's behavior. For example, Nader (1997c) notes that following a tornado, children reported more post-trauma stress symptoms for themselves than their teachers reported for them. Some children may become more focused on their schoolwork as well as quieter in the classroom. This type of change in behavior may be appreciated and go unreported.

Generic Therapies to Reduce the Effects of Trauma

As discussed in a previous chapter, crisis debriefing and related interventions can play a significant role in lessening some of the stressful effects of the trauma. Additionally, referrals to a professional trained in the use of one or more of the newer generic therapies can be extremely beneficial in reducing, and in many cases, eliminating troubling symptoms that present obstacles to the adjustment process. These therapies include:

- Eye Movement Desensitization and Reprocessing (EMDR)
- Thought Field Therapy (TFT)
- Visual Kinesthetic Disassociation (V/KD)
- Traumatic Incident Reduction (TIR)

These therapies have been empirically shown to be powerful, efficient, and effective. They take relatively little time, draw from both the work of traumatology and thanatology, and can be used with children as well as adults. Symptoms most often presenting barriers to adaptation revolve around personal vulnerability (e.g., fears, phobias, and terror), undue responsibility for the event (e.g., guilt, self-blame, depression), issues related to control (e.g., helplessness, powerlessness), horrific images, and anxiety in general. In easing the suffering from traumatic exposure, appropriate use of these therapies helps to promote the natural process of grieving. Although it is true that the sooner individuals receive generic therapies following the trauma, the more the suffering can be minimized (e.g., within the first few weeks following the violence), significant success has been recorded long after the event (Callahan & Callahan, 1997; Figley, 1996; Solomon & Shapiro, 1997). Generic therapies, however, are not "miracle cures." Rather, they can be an extremely beneficial part of an overall recovery plan.

Facilitating Understanding and Healing

In the face of so much helplessness, victims and co-victims will need to feel empowered. Being informed can help people become empowered. Knowledge about the following will be especially beneficial:

- Factual, accurate information as to what happened, what was/is being done, etc.
- What might be expected of and coping with the media
- Investigative proceedings and other relevant information about the criminal justice system
- Traumatic reactions
- The grief process
- Reactions and needs of children
- Interventions for children
- Second wounds
- Available services

Keep in mind that when people are in shock, confused and generally angry, they are experiencing considerable anxiety and will not have the tolerance or ability to absorb large amounts of data at first. Prioritizing what or how much is presented when, in what way (e.g., orally or in written form), and by whom should be a part of the overall crisis plan. Scheduling open meetings with parents, students, and for the general community is recommended. Developing an information bank during the planning stages can be helpful with dissemination of information in the days and weeks following a crisis. Information can include pamphlets and handouts on grieving, post-traumatic reactions, children's needs, etc. One school instituted a newsletter after a disaster to keep parents apprised of services for children and other developments (Nader & Pynoos, 1993).

Becoming actively involved in recovery efforts can prove beneficial to countering some of the helplessness. Students, for example, can make cards or bring food for the injured and bereaved, conduct fundraising efforts, provide input into any memorial or commemorative services planned, etc. Participation in peer support groups can also serve to lessen feelings of helplessness.

The verbiage used when communicating with survivors and bereaved family members can be influential in the adaptation process and in preventing second wounds. Use of death words, actual descriptive words such as "died," "killed," and "murdered" helps to confront reality (Redmond, 1989; Spungen, 1998). The person(s) who died did not "pass away." His death wasn't a peaceful passing from this world to the next. It was violent, unexpected, and worst of all, at the hands of another human being. The dead person(s) did not "expire." Licenses expire. Attempts to minimize the death and the way it happened can generate anger, perhaps fury, from survivors.

In the legal sense, a homicide was committed. Overuse of the term, however, allows people to distance themselves from the reality of murder. Most people cannot fathom the possibility of murder happening in their network of loved ones and friends, or to children. When such an atrocity does occur, survivors may be unable to comprehend the reality. The word "murder" is too threatening to even say. It seems to get stuck somewhere inside. But gentle usage of actual descriptive terms by others helps those affected to face the reality of death and the murder, and to begin the long process of healing.

Similarly, the proper name of murder victims should be used (Redmond, 1989). The person who died was cared for and loved by others. He had value and meaning. The dead should not be referred to as "it," or "the body," or only by pronouns such as him, her, etc.

Victims and co-victims of the violence will need validation and normalization for what they are experiencing. They will need reassurance that their reactions are not uncommon, that they are not abnormal; rather, it is the violence and the murder that is abnormal.

Above all, patience with one's self and with others is essential to the healing process. Adapting to any loss, much less murder and violence, takes longer than most people realize. Individuals will proceed at the rate and in the way they each need. Every person has his or her own journey. Some will have a longer road ahead than others and may require extra support or assistance as they traverse it.

As noted previously, following a catastrophe in which many are injured and killed, holding various open meetings to allow process reactions, provide information, and dispel rumors is essential. In addition to those held with school personnel and the student body, a meeting with parents and students prior to the reopening of the school can help to reduce some fears, ensure a sense of safety, and encourage students to return to classes. Scheduling an open meeting for the community as soon as reasonably possible is recommended. This has proven especially effective in relatively small communities (Pitcher & Poland, 1992; Poland, 1998b). If the event occurs at week's end, experience of some schools indicates that a meeting should be held during the weekend. Waiting until Monday has the potential for increasing confusion, chaos, and animosity towards the school. Additional meetings with parents and families can be scheduled as the situation warrants.

It is best if an outside mental health consultant facilitates the initial open meeting with parents and the community. Being less affected by the trauma and more objective, this person will be better able to provide a sense of calm. Administrators, crisis team members, and any other personnel participating in the meeting need to brace themselves for the intensity of reactions likely from attendees. In particular, the anger can become palpable and directed nearly everywhere—at the assailant, the assailant's family, the school, the police, the legal system, the government, etc. It will be important to keep the meeting under control. Some of the intensity can be defused by acknowledging feelings and focusing the group's energies away from blame and potential scapegoating and toward restoring normalcy, returning the children to school, and promoting healing.

When the trauma is large scale and occurs in the spring, it is beneficial if the school is kept open during the summer months for counseling and support group meetings. Such was the experience at the Cleveland Elementary School in Stockton, California, in 1989 when a gunman opened fire on a crowded playground. Five children were killed, and 29 students and one teacher were injured (Pitcher & Poland, 1992).

In classrooms strongly affected by the trauma, teachers may question how they can conduct normal classroom activities and continue to meet the needs of traumatized, grieving students. Confining classroom discussion of the incident to specified times gives young people an opportunity to process reactions while still going about the business of learning required academic material. It also allows teachers to remain within their roles without becoming therapists (Nader & Pynoos, 1993).

Cultural Influences

In communities where there is considerable cultural diversity, large populations of a particular culture, and/or one or more of those killed or injured representing a culture differing from the majority, attention must be given to language barriers and to differing beliefs and practices. For example, speaking directly of the dead or of death itself is taboo for some Native Americans and Asians. Some groups, such as the Hmong from Southeast Asia, may adhere to traditional folk medicine and rituals, which will need to be honored and respected. Seeking input from members of differing cultures during the planning phases and for interventions (including any commemorative services) following a crisis will help minimize difficulties and promote healing. Where appropriate, these individuals should be part of the Crisis Response Team.

The Site of the Violence

A number of issues concerning the site of the violence and killing are of importance. First, police will have it cordoned off for a period of time as they conduct investigations of the crime scene. As soon as possible, cleanup of blood and such will be necessary. This may be best left to professional cleaning services rather than to school maintenance personnel. These staff members may have been at the scene during the violence, knew those who were killed, and are experiencing their own reactions to the trauma. Including names and phone numbers of professional cleaning agencies in the Crisis Response Plan will save time and anxiety in the event of an actual violent episode.

Some of those with direct traumatic exposure, family members of victims, and others may need a visit to the site of the tragedy as a way of making it real in trying to make sense of it. It is helpful if school officials are understanding of this need and are able to accommodate it in ways that will not be disruptive to regular school activities. On the other hand, some of those directly traumatized at the time of the event may temporarily avoid the site where the carnage took place lest it bring back the terror. These feelings, too, require respect and understanding. Recognizing these needs can be included in meetings for faculty, staff, students, their parents, and the general community.

Differing Needs: Those with Direct Trauma Exposure and Those Who Are Grieving

At times, the needs of those who were at the site of the trauma during the violence and those bereaved by the deaths may clash. Awareness of and sensitivity to these differences can help to minimize problems. Compromise and solutions are possible when people are aware of each other's needs, open communication is fostered, and input from both sides is solicited (Nader, 1997b).

For example, when murder occurs in a public place, the crime scene is sometimes made into a temporary shrine where others come to reflect, perhaps say a prayer, and leave flowers, candles, and various mementos. This can be therapeutic to mourners, helping to facilitate the grieving process. Developing permanent memorials at the school, however, must be done with the differing needs of the bereaved and of the traumatized in mind.

Bereaved family and friends are likely to want a variety of reminders of those slain in the incident. They do not want their loved ones to be forgotten. For the directly traumatized, too many visible reminders or those obviously symbolizing the violence (or perceived as such) are also reminders of the chaos, the sound of bullets, the cries for help, the blood, and the carnage. Commemorative reminders may serve to interfere with the ability of some students, teachers, staff, and others to function adequately in their respective roles. The needs of both sides can be met with open discussion and mutual input. Plaques, sculptures, and other commemorative items can be developed so that those who died are honored while symbols of the violence are minimized.

Differing needs of these two groups may also emerge in support groups. Either group may feel disenfranchised because of the profound needs and reactions of the other group. Those traumatized may experience further intensification of symptoms such as survivor guilt and feelings of responsibility when bereaved survivors discuss the magnitude of their loss and grief.

When the Assailant is a Student

When the assailant is a student at the school where the killings took place, he may have had siblings and friends who are students at the school. These children are of special concern. Siblings, in particular, are very likely to be the targets of misdirected anger and blame by other students, and unfortunately, some adults. Both siblings and friends may be questioned by police during the course of investigations. Their own friends may turn away, and they may have to endure taunting by other children. Guilt and shame will be compounded for these young people. Their sense of isolation and disenfranchisement may be especially acute as their need to openly express their feelings is thwarted. As a result, they may withdraw into a depression, act out their pain, or become overachievers.

These children will also be in need of support and understanding. Special care must be given to them, and precautions should be taken to minimize the stigma they will endure. Other students must be helped to understand that the answer to "why" may never be fully known, that siblings and friends of the perpetrator were not necessarily to blame, and that they are also suffering. The teacher might encourage students to show concern for these children by making them cards, telephoning them, and including them in various activities. These children must be given ample opportunity to express and process their myriad of reactions in a supportive, nonjudgmental atmosphere.

The Aftermath:
Providing Support and Assistance to School Personnel

In the aftermath of a violent, catastrophic event, the school atmosphere will be different for a period of time. Anxiety, fear, and feelings of victimization may dominate as individuals contend with their own traumatic reactions. Everyone at the school will be vulnerable to reminders of the trauma (e.g., loud noises, the site of the violence, etc.). In the midst of all this, demands and responsibilities of school personnel will increase.

Office staff will experience a significant increase in paperwork as well as telephone calls and in-person intrusions from the media, family members, outside consultants, concerned community members, etc. Nurturing support staff may be the first people some students and others turn to when looking for a listening ear or a source of comfort. Yet, these people are generally not trained to respond to the distress. Hiring temporary office and support staff to assist existing staff is likely to be warranted.

Referrals to and duties of the nursing, counseling, and related offices substantially increase following a trauma. Depending on the extent of the caseloads, hiring temporary assistants for some of these personnel may be necessary.

Principals will need to take strong leadership roles if there is to be recovery within the school. The principal and other administrators will be called upon to deal with the anger, anxiety, demands, and concerns of parents and the wider community in the aftermath of the traumatic event. Because of their leadership role, administrators are at high risk for a delayed response sometime after normalcy returns to the school. It is recommended that appropriate psychological services be available for school leaders once routine operations have resumed (Nader & Pynoos, 1993).

The very nature of the role that teachers play in the lives of young people renders them especially vulnerable to being intensely traumatized as the result of the violent death of students. One study showed that teachers at a school where a child was shot and killed reported reaction levels similar to widowed persons during the first year of bereavement (Nader & Pynoos, 1993). Relief from some duties (e.g., committee work, lunch duty, etc.) and the use of teaching assistants or substitute teachers as classroom aides may be helpful for those most affected (Pitcher & Poland, 1992).

Those providing the most care at the time of a crisis are often the ones who are most overlooked for needing care in its aftermath. In the days following the incident, the crisis team will continue to be looked to for advice, support, and assistance. Debriefing following the crisis is essential and must be part of the overall Crisis Response Plan. When the crisis involves large numbers of people and is of a violent nature, follow-up team meetings for supportive purposes and continued debriefing will be needed.

Overall, to prevent exacerbation of symptoms and burnout of various school personnel, and to facilitate recovery for the school community, Nader and Pynoos (1993) recommend the following:

- Evaluate traumatic responses
- Allow personnel to have ongoing debriefing or related care in the course of their work
- Minimize and/or adjust workloads (hire temporary help where needed)
- Give permission to step out of the post-trauma interventions if special tasks are too much
- Give direct, visible support and assistance from school superintendents

☐ Every School Should Be Prepared

Although statistically a rare event, any school could become the site of violence and killing. The incidence of these events has increased in recent years. Schools can choose to ignore this and hope for the best, or they can be prepared. They can take steps towards the prevention of violence as well as develop a comprehensive Crisis Intervention Plan. Updating of the plan, periodic in-service training, and crisis drills for the Crisis Response Team will help to ensure the plan's effectiveness, should it be needed. Incorporating strategies and interventions such as those suggested in this chapter, and throughout this book, can help to make the school a site of healing should a violent, tragic incident occur. In so doing, community trust and confidence in the school will be restored.

APPENDIX

Anti-Violence Partnership (AVP) of Philadelphia
1421 Arch Street
Philadelphia, PA 19102
(215) 686-8033

Association for Death Education and Counseling (ADEC)
638 Prospect Avenue
Hartford, CT 06105
(860) 586-7503

Center for the Prevention of School Violence
20 Enterprise Street, Suite 2
Raleigh, NC 27606-7375
(919) 515-9397
(800) 299-6054

Families of Murder Victims (FMV) Program
1421 Arch Street
Philadelphia, PA 19102
(215) 686-8033

International Critical Incident Stress Foundation
10176 Baltimore National Pike, Unit 201
Ellicott City, MD 21042
(410) 750-9600
24-hour hotline: (410) 313-2473

National Association of State Boards of Education
Publications
1-12 Cameron Street
Alexandria, VA 22314

National Hospice Organization (NHO)
1901 N. Moore Street, Suite 901
Arlington, VA 22209-1714
(703) 243-5900

National Organization of Victims Assistance (NOVA)
1757 Park Road NW
Washington, DC 20010
(202) 232-6632

National Victim Center (NVC)
2111 Wilson Boulevard, Suite 300
Arlington, VA 22201
(703) 276-2880

Parents of Murdered Children (POMC)
100 East 8th Street, Suite B-41
Cincinnati, OH 54202
(513) 721-5683

REFERENCES

Alberta Canada Minister of Education. (1992). *Bereavement and loss manual for administrators and teachers*. Alberta, Canada: Author.

American Psychiatric Association. (1994). *Diagnostic and statistical manual of mental disorders*. (4th ed.). Washington, DC: Author.

Bagge, R., & Brandsma, J. (1994). PTSD and bereavement: traumatic grief. In Hyer and Associates. *Trauma victim: Theoretical issues and practical suggestions*. Muncie, IN: Accelerated Development.

Bark, E. (1989, April 23). Imagemakers tell clients be honest with media. *Houston Chronicle*, p. 4E.

Bertois, J., & Allen, J. (1988). School Management of a Bereaved Child. *Elementary School Guidance and Counseling, 23*, 30–38.

Callahan, R., & Callahan, J. (1997). Thought field therapy: Aiding the bereavement process. In C. Figley, B. Bride, & N. Mazza (Eds.), *Death and trauma: The traumatology of grieving*. Washington, DC: Taylor & Francis.

Case, D. R., & Case, D. (1995). Responding to a bereaved child in the school setting. ERIC Document ED 394 655.

Cassini, K., & Rogers, J. (1991) *Death and the classroom*. Cincinnati: Griefwork of Cincinnati.

Connelly, M. (1992). *A student dies, a school mourns, are you prepared?* [Videotape]. Buffalo, NY: Thanos Institute.

Cook, A., & Oltijenbrums, K. (1989). *Dying and grieving: Lifespan and family perspective*. New York: Holt Rinehart and Winston.

Cunningham, B., & Hare, J. (1989). Essential elements of a teacher in-service program on child bereavement. *Elementary School Guidance and Counseling, 23*, 175–182.

Doherty, S. (1989, November 13). Teaching kids how to grieve. *Newsweek*, p. 73.

Doka, K. (1996). *Living with grief after sudden loss*. Washington, DC: Taylor & Francis.

Doka, K. (Ed.) (1989). *Disenfranchised grief: Recognizing hidden sorrow*. Lexington, MA: Lexington Books.

Doka, K. (Ed.) (1995). *Children mourning children*. Washington, DC: Hospice Association of America.

Doka, K. (Ed.). (1996). *Living with grief after sudden loss*. Washington, DC: Taylor & Francis.

Duncan, G. (1958). Etiological factors in first degree murder. *Journal of the American Medical Association, 168*, 1755–1758.

Eagen, T. (1998, June 14). From adolescent angst to school killings. *New York Times*.

Elder, S. (1994). Support groups in schools. In R. Stevenson (Ed.), *What will we do now? Preparing a school community to cope with crises*. Amityville, NY: Baywood.

Elliott, J. (1989, April 21). Public angry at slow action on oil spill. *USA Today*, p. 16.

Eth, S., & Pynoos, R. (Eds.). (1985). *Post-traumatic stress disorder in children*. Washington, DC: American Psychiatric Press.

Feinsilber, M. (1998, July 30). Kin's link to terrible deeds haunts families forever. *The Buffalo News.*

Figley, C., Bride, B., & Mazza, N. (Eds.). (1997). *Death and trauma: The traumatology of grieving.* Washington, DC: Taylor & Francis.

Figley, C. (1996). Traumatic death: Treatment implications. In K. Doka (Ed.), *Living with grief after sudden loss.* Washington, DC: Taylor & Francis.

Fitzgerald, H. (1992). *The grieving child: A parent's guide.* New York: Simon & Schuster.

Frantz, T. (1990). *Grief in a school community: A student dies, a school mourns, are you prepared?* [Teleseminar]. Buffalo, NY: Thanos Institute.

Frantz, T. (1997). *Grief in the workplace.* Speech presented at Circle of Hope Seminar, Lockport, NY.

Freud, S. (1957). Mourning and melancholia. In J. Strachey (Ed. and Trans.). *The standard edition of the complete psychological works of Sigmund Freud (Vol. 14).* London: Hogarth. (Original work published 1917).

Froggie, S. (1992). Dealing with sudden death. *Life Line,* 24–26.

Garbarino, J., Kostelny, K., & Dubrow, N. (1991). What children can tell us about living in danger. *American Psychologist, 46*(4), 376–383.

Giblin, N., & Ryan, F. (1991). Reaching the child's perception of death. In Morgan (Ed.), *Young People and Death.* Philadelphia: Charles Press.

Glass, C. (1990). Death, loss, and grief in high school students. *The High School Journal, 73,* 154–160.

Goldman, L. (1994). *Life and loss: A guide to help grieving children.* Washington, DC: Accelerated Development.

Goldman, L. (1996). *Breaking the silence: A guide to helping children with complicated grief—suicide, homicide, AIDS, violence, abuse.* Washington, DC: Accelerated Development.

Gorin, S. (1998, May 1–4). Crisis in Jonesboro. *Communiqué,*

Grollman, E. (1993). *Straight talk about death for teenagers.* Boston: Beacon.

Grollman, E. (Ed.). (1995). *Bereaved children and teens.* Boston: Beacon.

Haig, R. (1990). *The anatomy of grief: Biopsychological and therapeutic perspectives.* Springfield, IL: Charles C. Thomas.

Harris, M., & Lord, J. (1990). *Death at school: A guide for teachers, school nurses, counselors, and administrators.* Dallas: Mothers Against Drunk Driving.

Hasley, J. (1988). How to write letters of comfort to the bereaved. *The Director,* 12–14.

Hendriks, J., Black, D., & Kaplan, T. (1993). *When father kills mother: Guiding children through trauma and grief.* New York: Routledge.

Holland, J., & Ludford, C. (1995, June). The effects of bereavement on children in Humberside Secondary Schools. *British Journal of Special Education, 2,* 56–59.

Holland, J. (1993). Child bereavement in Humberside primary schools. *Educational Research, 35,* 289–296.

Irizarry, C. (1992). Spirituality and the child: A grandparent's death. In G. Cox & R. Fundis (Eds.), *Spiritual, ethical, and pastoral aspects of death and bereavement.* Amityville, NY: Baywood Publishing.

Jay, B. (1989). Managing a crisis in a school. *National Association of Secondary Schools Bulletin, 1,* 27.

Jenkins-Henry, J. (1993). *Just us: Overcoming and understanding homicidal loss and grief.* Omaha Centering Corporation, Omaha, NE: Centering Corporation..

Kaczmarek, V. (1998). *Grief: The universal experience.* Lackawanna, NY: Community Grief Center.

Klicker, R. (1993). *A student dies, a school mourns, are you prepared?* Buffalo, NY: Thanos Institute.

Klicker, R. (1997). *The Klicker study.* Buffalo, NY: Thanos Institute.

Kline, M., Schonfeld, D., & Lichtenstein, R. (1995, September). Benefits and challenges of school-based crisis response teams. *Journal of School Health, 65*(7), 245–249.

Kohly, M. (1994). *Reported child abuse and neglect victims during the flood months of 1993*. St. Louis, MO: Missouri Department of Social Services, Division of Family Services, Research and Development Unit.

Kroen, W. (1996). *Helping children cope with the loss of a loved one: A guide for growing*. Minneapolis: Free Spirit.

Lichtenstein, R., Schonfeld, D., & Kline, M. (1994, November). School crisis response: Expecting the unexpected. *Educational Leadership, 52*(3), 79–83.

Lindemann, E. (1944). Symptomology and management of acute grief. *American Journal of Psychiatry 101*, 141–148.

Lipton, H. (1990). Crisis in New York City Schools Symposium. Presented at the meeting of the National Association of School Psychologists. San Francisco.

Lord, J. (1996). America's number one killer. In K. Doka (Ed.), *Vehicular crashes and living with grief after sudden loss*. Washington, DC: Taylor & Francis.

McCann, I., & Pearlman, L. (1990). Vicarious traumatization: A framework for understanding the psychological effects of working with victims. *Journal of Traumatic Stress, 3*(1), 131–149.

McIntyre, M., & Reid, B. (1989). *Obstacles to implementation of crisis intervention programs*. Unpublished manuscript. Chesterfield, VA: Chesterfield County Schools.

Morgan, J. (1990). *The dying and bereaved teenager*. Philadelphia: Charles Press.

Morgan, J. (Ed.). (1995). *Personal care in an impersonal world: A multi-dimensional look at bereavement*. Amityville, NY: Baywood Publishing.

Nader, K. (1997a). Childhood traumatic loss: The interaction of trauma and grief. In C. Figley, B. Bride, & N. Mazza (Eds.), *Death and trauma: The traumatology of grieving*. Washington, DC: Taylor & Francis.

Nader, K. (1997b). Treating traumatic grief in systems. In C. Figley, B. Bride, & N. Mazza (Eds.), *Death and trauma: The traumatology of grieving*. Washington, DC: Taylor & Francis.

Nader, K. (1997c). Assessing traumatic experiences in children. In J. Wilson & T. Keane (Eds.), *Assessing psychological trauma and PTSD*. New York: Guilford Press.

Nader, K., & Pynoos, R. (1993). School disaster: Planning and initial interventions. In R. Allen (Ed.), *Journal of Social Behavior and Personality, 8*(5), 299–320.

Naierman, N. (1997, October). Reaching out to grieving students. *Educational Leadership*, 62–64.

New York Times. (1998, April 7). Sex abuse is claimed in school slayings case. *New York Times*. National Desk Section, p.

Newberger, E., & Newberger, C. (1992). Treating children who witness violence. In D. Schwartz (Ed.), *Children and violence report of the 23rd Ross roundtable on critical approaches to common pediatric problems*, pp. 87–97. Columbus, OH: Ross Laboratories.

Newton, R. (1990). *Children in the funeral ritual: Factors that affect their attendance and participation*. M.S. thesis, California State University, Chico.

Oates, M. (1988). Responding to death in the schools. *Texas Association for Counselors Developmental Journal, 16*(2), 83–86.

Obiakor, F., Mehring, T., & Schwenn, J. (1977). *Distruption, disasters and death: Helping students deal with crisis*. Reston, VA: The Council of Exceptional Children.

Overbeck, B., & Overbeck, J. (1992). *Helping children cope with loss*. Dallas: TLC Group.

Parachin, V. (1998, February). How our friends helped after a death to suicide. *The Director*, p. 4, 6, 8.

Pennells, M., & Smith, S. (1995). *The forgotten mourners*. London: Jessica Kingsley.

Perea, R., & Morrison, S. (1997, October). Preparing for a crisis. *Educational Leadership*, 42–43.

Phillips, D., & Carstensen, L. (1989). Clustering of teenage suicide after television news stories about suicide. *New England Journal of Medicine, 3*(15), 685–689.

Pitcher, G., & Poland, S. (1992). *Crisis Intervention in the schools*. New York: Guilford Press.

Poland, G., & Pitcher, G. (1990). Best practices in crisis intervention. In A. Thomas & J. Gunne (Eds.), *Best Practices in School Psychology* (Vol. 2, 259–275). Washington, DC: National Association of School Psychologists.

Poland, S. (1998a, May 5). NEAT chairman leads NOVA team in Paducah. *Communiqué*, p.

Poland, S. (1998b, June 4–5). Jonesboro turns to school psychologists for leadership. *Communiqué*, p. 4.

Postel, C. (1986). Death in my classroom. *Teaching Exceptional Children*, 139–43.

Preller, P. (1994, October). Developing an emergency response plan helps schools prepare for crises. *The Regional Lab Reports*, 4.

Rando, T. (1993). *Treatment of complicated mourning.* Champaign, IL: Research Press.

Rando, T. (1988). *Grieving: How to go on living when someone you love dies.* Lexington, MA: Lexington Books.

Raphael, B. (1986). *When disaster strikes: How individuals and communities cope with catastrophe.* New York: Basic Books.

Redmond, L. (1989). *Surviving: When someone you love was murdered.* Clearwater, FL: Psychological Consultation and Education Services.

Redmond, L. (1990). *Surviving when someone you loved was murdered.* Clearwater, FL: Clearwater Psychological Consultation and Educational Services.

Ressler, R., & Burgess, A. (1985). The men who murdered. *FBI Law Enforcement Bulletin, 54*, 2–6.

Ritter, R. (1994). Critical incident stress debriefing teams. In R. Stevenson (Ed.),. *Preparing a school community to cope with crises.* Amityville, New York: Baywood.

Rosen, E. (1990). *Families facing death: Family dynamics of terminal illness.* New York: Lexington Books.

Schaefer, D., & Lyons, C. (1986). *How do we tell the children?* New York: Newmarket Press.

Schonfeld, D. (1993). Talking with children about death. *Journal of Pediatric Health Care,* 269–274.

Simpson, M. (1997). Traumatic bereavements and death-related PTSD. In C. Figley, B. Bride, & N. Mazza (Eds.), *Death and trauma: The traumatology of grieving.* Washington, DC: Taylor & Francis.

Sinkkonen, M. (1989, May/June). Responding sensitively to tragedy. *Thrust, 22.*

Snyder, T. D. (1993). When tragedy strikes. *Executive Educatior 15*(7), 30–31.

Solomon, R., & Shapiro, F. (1997). Eye movement desensitization and reprocessing: A therapeutic tool for trauma and grief. In C. Figley, B. Bride, & N. Mazza (Eds.), *Death and trauma: The traumatology of grieving.* Washington, DC: Taylor & Francis.

Spungen, D. (1998). *Homocide: The hidden victims.* Thousand Oaks, CA: Sage.

Stevens, R. (1990, Fall). Don't get caught with your pants down. *National School Safety Journal,* 4–8.

Stevenson, R. (Ed.). (1994). *What will we do? Preparing a school community to cope with crises.* Amityville, NY: Baywood.

Stevenson, R., & Powers, H. (1987). How to handle death in school. *The Education Digest, 52,* 42–43.

Terr, L. (1991). Childhood traumas: An outline and overview. *American Journal of Psychiatry, 148*(1), 10–20.

van der Kolk, B. (1989). The compulsion to repeat the trauma: Re-enactment, revictimization, and masochism. *Psychiatric Clinics of North America, 12,* 389–411.

van der Kolk, B., & Saporta, J. (1991). The biological response to psychic trauma: Mechanisms and treatment of intrusion and numbing. *Anxiety Research, 4,* 199–212.

Wilson, J., & Keane, T. (1997). *Assessing psychological trauma and PTSD.* New York: Guilford Press.

Wilson, J., & Raphael, B. (Eds.). (1993). *International handbook of traumatic stress syndromes.* New York: Plenum.

Wiseman, B. (1998). Each grief is unique. *Bereavement Magazine,* 32–33.

Wolfelt, A. (1983). *Helping children with grief.* Washington, DC: Accelerated Development.

Wolfelt, A. (1991, December). Understanding adolescent mourning. *American Funeral Director,* 49–52.

Wolfelt, A. (1995). Helping grieving children at school. *Bereavement Magazine,* 10–11.

Worden, W. (1996). *Children and grief.* New York: Guilford Press.

Wrobleski, A. (1994). *Suicide: Survivors, a guide for those left behind* (2nd edition). Minneapolis, MN: Afterwords.

Wrobleski, A. (1995). *Suicide: Why? 85 questions and answers about suicide* (2nd edition). Minneapolis, MN: Afterwords.

AUTHOR INDEX

SUBJECT INDEX

139

ABOUT THE AUTHOR

Ralph L. Klicker is president of the Thanos Institute in Buffalo, New York, a continuing education organization specializing in death-related studies. He has been involved in the field of death and dying for over thirty years in various capacities, and has held positions including funeral director, executive director of a grief-related counseling center, assistant professor, and college dean. His experiences led him to produce an international teleseminar on death in the school community. He is the author of a children's book on death and funerals, which has attained wide readership in North America, Great Britain, and Australia. His other books on death and grief including *Funeral Directing and Funeral Service Management* and *Ethics in Funeral Service*.

N